Standard Grade
ENGLISH
Credit

John Seely
David Kitchen
Gordon Gibson
Anne Gifford

Heinemann

Heinemann Educational Publishers
Halley Court, Jordan Hill, Oxford OX2 8EJ
A division of Reed Educational and Professional Publishing Ltd

**OXFORD MELBOURNE AUCKLAND
JOHANNESBURG BLANTYRE GABORONE IBADAN
PORTSMOUTH (NH) USA CHICAGO**

This edition first published 2002

06 05 04 03 02
10 9 8 7 6 5 4 3 2 1

ISBN 0 435 10922 7

Original design by Gecko Ltd

Designed and produced by Gecko Limited, Bicester, Oxon.

Original illustrations © Heinemann Educational Publishers, 2002

Illustrations by Gerry Ball, Paul Davies, Paul Hampson, Pantelis Palios,
Brian Smith, Jamie Sneddon, Sam Thompson, Katherine Walker,
Dave Wood, Kathryn Prewett and Alice Englander.

Printed and bound in Spain by Printer Trento

Acknowledgements

The publishers gratefully acknowledge the following for permission to reproduce copyright material.
Every effort has been made to trace copyright holders, but in some cases this has proved impossible.
The publishers would be happy to hear from any copyright holder who has not been acknowledged.

Article 'Coul: I would rather crash than wimp out' by Stan Piecha, in *The Sun*, Tuesday, 3 April 2001.
Copyright © News International Newspapers Limited, 3 April 2001. Used with permission (p. 11); Extract
from article 'Victory brings extra burden for Coulthard' by Stuart Bathgate, *The Scotsman*, Tuesday, 3
April 2001. Reprinted with permission (p. 11); 'Watch out, there's a granny about' by Tabitha
Troughton. Reprinted by permission of *The Spectator* 1828 Limited (p. 13–15); Extract from *Not So
Stupid!* by Malorie Blackman, published in Great Britain by The Women's Press Limited, 1990, 34 Great
Sutton Street, London EC1V 0LQ, used by permission of the Women's Press Limited (p. 17); Extract from
'Pitmedden Folk' by James Allan Ford from *The Devil and The Giro*, edited by Carl MacDougall and
published by Canongate Books Limited, Edinburgh in 1991. Reprinted by permission (p. 18); 'This Year'
by Ron Butlin, found in *The Ghost of Liberace*, edited by Al Kennedy & Hamish Whyte, ASLS 1993.
Reprinted with the kind permission of the poet (p. 19); Headline 'Desolate Graf talks of Ordeal' from *The
Independent*, 17 October 1995. Reprinted with permission of The Independent, Syndication (p. 20);
Headline 'Steffi, laughing off $1m loss', from *Daily Mail*, 17 October 1995. Reprinted with permission of
Atlantic Syndication (p. 20); Extract from article 'TV Licence shocker' from *Daily Mirror*, 16 October
1995. Reprinted by permission of Mirror Syndications (p. 21); Extract 'Only players can stop the dives'
by Stephen McGowan, from *Daily Mail*, Wednesday, 20 September 2000. Reprinted with permission of
Atlantic Syndication (p. 22); Article 'Still smiling aged 120' from *Daily Express*, 16 October 1995;
'Noble art is man's right' by Julian Critchley, Conservative MP for Aldershot, *Daily Express*, 16 October
1995; and 'Time to ring the last bell' by Dr Vivienne Nathanson, Head of Policy, BMA, *Daily Express*, 16
October 1995. Reprinted with permission of Daily Express Syndications (pp. 22, 50, 51); Article 'We
send in the girls' from *The Sun*, 31 May 1995. Copyright © News International Newspapers Limited, 31
May 1995. Used with permission (p. 22); 'Avila is the highest city in Spain' by James Bentley, from *Hello!*
Magazine. Reprinted by permission of *Hello!* Magazine (pp. 26, 45); Letter from 'A. Lawrie Morton, Royal
Alexandra Hospital, Paisley' headed 'A great scandal of the modern NHS' from *The Herald*, 18 June
2001. Reprinted by permission of SMG Newspapers Limited (p. 27); Extract from 'Dreams in Cold
Storage' by Kay Carmichael, from *Meantime: An Anthology of Women's Writings*, published by
Polygon in 1991. Reprinted with the kind permission of the author (p. 27); 'Dominican Republic Travel
Notes' from *BBC Holidays* Magazine, March 1995. Reprinted with permission of BBC Magazines (p. 28);
Extract from *Toxic waste and recycling* by Nigel Hawkes, published by Aladdin Books, 1988 (Franklin
Watts), (p. 29); Extract from *Rubbish* by Claire Llewellyn, published by MacDonald Young Books (p. 30);
'If you were in Northern France during the third week of June....' by Simon Taylor, from *BBC Worldwide*
Magazine, June 1995. © BBC Worldwide 1995. Reprinted by permission of BBC Magazines (p. 31);
Extract from article 'Dummy runs that end in death' by Iain Wilson, from *The Herald*, 2 April 2001.
Reprinted by permission of SMG Newspapers Limited (p. 36); Extract from *An Indian Summer* by
James Cameron. Reprinted by permission of David Higham Associates Limited (p. 37); 'The Drawer' by
George MacBeth Copyright © George MacBeth. Reprinted by permission of Sheil Land Associates Limited
(p. 38); Extract from *Scottish Journey* by Edwin Muir, published by Faber and Faber (p. 45); Extract
from *The Old Patagonian Express: By Train Through the Americas* by Paul Theroux (Hamish
Hamilton, 1979) Copyright © Cape Cod Scriveners Co, 1979. Reprinted by permission of Penguin Books
Limited (p. 45); Extract 'Master offers chance to be an Ettrick shepherd for the weekend' by William
Chisholm, from *The Scotsman*, 2 November 2000. Reprinted with permission (p. 57); Extract from
Writing an Article by Brendan Hennessy, published by How To Books Limited, Oxford. Reprinted with
permission of the publishers (p. 59); 'War Games' by Caroline Elliott, from *Focus* Magazine. Reprinted by
permission of National Magazine Company (p. 60); Extract from *Secrets* by Bernard MacLaverty,
published by Blackstaff Press. Reprinted by permission of Blackstaff Press Limited (pp. 63–5); Extract
from *A Gun For Sale* by Graham Greene, published by Random House. Reprinted by permission of David
Higham Associates Limited (pp. 66–8); Extract from 'Tutti Frutti' from *Into the Ebb* by Christopher
Rush. Reprinted with the kind permission of the author (p. 71); Extract from *Countdown* by Alan
Ayckbourn. Copyright © 1970 by Alan Ayckbourn. All rights whatsoever in this play are strictly reserved
and application for performance etc must be made before rehearsal to Casarotto Ramsay & Associates

Limited, National House, 60–66 Wardour Street, London WIV 4ND. No performance may be given unless
a licence has been obtained (pp. 74–5); Extract from *Elizabeth Gordon Quinn* by Chris Hannan, from
Scot-Free: New Scottish Plays, published by Nick Hern Books in 1990. Reprinted by permission of Nick
Hern Books (pp. 76–7); Extract from 'Above the Dock' by T. E. Hulme from *Speculations*, published by
Routledge & Kegan Paul. Reprinted by permission of Taylor & Francis (p. 79); 'The Gowdan Ba' and
'Ballad' by William Soutar. Reprinted with permission of National Library of Scotland (pp. 80, 130); 'A
Mean Wind' by Edwin Morgan, from *Collected Poems*, published by Carcanet Press. Reprinted by
permission of Carcanet Press Limited (p. 85); 'John Godber: I've been an outsider since the 11 plus' by
Dannie Danziger, *The Independent*, 21 March 1994. Reprinted by permission of The Independent
Syndications (p. 87); Extract from *Dark Child* by Camara Laye, published by HarperCollins Publishers
Limited (p. 88); Extract from *Stone Cold* by Robert Swindells (Hamish Hamilton, 1993) Copyright ©
Robert Swindells 1993. Reprinted by permission of Penguin Books Limited (pp. 92–3, 94); Extract from
Off the Rails by Lisa St Aubin de Teran. Copyright © Lisa St Aubin de Teran. Reprinted by permission of
A. M. Heath & Co. Ltd (p. 98); 'Kelly Wood' by Charles Causley, from *Collected Poems*, published by
Macmillan. Reprinted by permission of David Higham Associates Limited (pp. 100, 101); 'Roadgang
Women' by Valerie Gillies. Reprinted with the kind permission of the author (p. 102); Extracts from
Young People and Drinking – a Guide for Parents, reproduced by permission of The Portman Group,
London W1M 9DE (pp. 108–11); 'Interview with Jeremy Irons' by Lynn Barber, from *Mostly Men* by
Lynn Barber, published by Viking. Copyright © Lynn Barber. Reprinted by permission of Rogers,
Coleridge & White Limited, 20 Powis Mews, London W11 1JN (pp. 133–7); *A Piece of Wood* by Ray
Bradbury. Copyright © 1952 by Esquire Inc., renewed 1980 by Ray Bradbury. Reprinted by permission of
Don Congdon Associates Inc. (pp. 138–42); Extracts from Alan Bennett's *Talking Heads*, reproduced
with the permission of BBC Worldwide Limited. Copyright © Alan Bennett 1988 (pp. 145–8; pp.
149–53); Extract from *Growing Up in the 60s* by Cecile Landau, published by Vermilion. Used by
permission of The Random House Group Limited (p. 165); ''Member 'At' by Bill Bryden, as featured in
Jock Tamson's *Bairns: Essays on a Scots Childhood*, edited by Trevor Royle and published by Hamish
Hamilton in 1977 (p. 168); Extract from *Country Days* by Alice Taylor, published by Brandon Publishers
(p. 171); Extract from *In Search of our Mothers' Gardens* by Alice Walker, published by The Women's
Press. Reprinted by permission of David Higham Associates Limited (p. 171); Extract from *Family* by
Susan Hill, published by Michael Joseph. Copyright © Susan Hill. Reprinted by permission of Sheil Land
Associates Limited (p. 171); Extract from *A Childhood in Scotland* by Christian Miller, published by
John Murray. Reprinted by permission of John Murray (Publishers) Limited (p. 171); Extract from
A House in Flanders by Michael Jenkins, published by Souvenir Press (p. 171); 'We can build a better
world' by Richard Collins, found in *Wales on Sunday*. Reprinted with permission (p. 177).

The publishers and authors would also like to thank the following copyright holders for permission to
reproduce photographs on the pages noted below: Associated Press/Dario Lopez-Mills, p. 10 (left); PA
Photos, p. 10 (right); Allsport, p. 20; Heinemann, p. 23 (left), 167 ; Barnaby's Picture Library /Herb Parkin
(p. 23 right); Impact/ Christopher Cormack, p. 28 (top); NHPA/A.N.T., p. 28(middle); John Seely, pp. 42,
43, 46, 47, 127 (top, bottom left), 173, 181, 182, 183, 184, 185, 186, 187, 188, 189, 190, 191; Rex
Features/ Tim Rooke, p. 52; Malcolm Cochrane, p. 57; Rex Features, pp. 98, 133, 165; Missouri Historical
Society, St Louis, p. 104; Barnaby's Picture Library/D. Storey, p. 121 (top left); SCOPE, pp. 121 (bottom
right), 124 ; Volkswagen Group UK Ltd/ Skoda, pp. 122, 123; Barnaby's Picture Library, p. 126 (top left);
Popperfoto/Vernon D. Shaw, p. 126 (top left); Barnaby's Picture Library/ Alan Felix, p. 126 (bottom right);
Barnaby's Picture Library/M. D. Turner, p. 126 (bottom left); John Birdsall Photography, p. 127 (bottom
right); Rex Features/ Richard Young, p. 135; Rex Features/The Sun, p. 166 (top left); Rex Features/ Brian
Rasic, p. 166 (top right); Rex Features/ Ammar and Robbo, p. 166 (middle right); Warner Bros, p. 166
(bottom right), John Seely and David Kitchen would like to thank the following people for their help with
the original edition of this book (1996):

- Adrian Wombwell, shipwright
- Teachers and students at Glyn Derw High School, Cardiff
- Rachel Yeats, Gavin Anderson, Patsy Sterling, K. I. C. K., the people of Kisumu Jua Kali and the staff at
  VSO, Kisumu
- Staff at VSO, London, especially Silke Bernau
- Tony Farrell and Karen Lewis–Jones for their detailed and helpful assessment of the manuscript.

Introduction and contents

Standard Grade English is a comprehensive resource for Standard Grade. It ensures you will have the skills to complete your folio course work and your examinations with confidence; it contains lively and imaginative material which we hope you will enjoy using.

Section A introduces and consolidates the skills you require for effective reading, writing, talking, listening and critical evaluation.

Section B offers longer units for exam practice and coursework.

Section A contents

This section introduces and practises the skills you need for effective reading, writing, and response to literature.

An approach to reading

An approach to writing

Forms of writing

Approaching literature

A1 Reading

In the course of a day you read many different kinds of material and for many different reasons.

How would you describe the purpose for reading each of these texts?

A

Dig out 7.5 cm–10 cm of soil. Rake the surface level and roll or tread firm. If the soil is not firm enough, you will need to roll in a layer of hardcore and then even this up with a layer of sand. The important thing is to achieve a firm, level surface on which to lay the slabs.

B

The building didn't seem very promising. Melanie fished the letter out of her bag and looked at it again. It definitely said, 'Scalloway House, 2nd floor'. The letter went on, 'Ask for Mr Yeading. On no account mention the name of Vin Dyce.' She put the letter in her bag and went up to the second floor.

D

IN 1235 NAVARRE, the widow of Stephen of Servian, arrived at the fortress. She had already been appointed an elder of the heretical sect, the Cathars, and during the campaign of 1227–8 she had visited Alamain de Rouaix in Toulouse. Now she had come to Montségur to die.

C

It was great to see you and Hannah again after such a long time. And Baby Mark is just the spitting image of his dad! Now we've got together again we mustn't leave it so long before meeting again. I was wondering if you'd like to come over here next time.

F

Today's choice

Five down and two to play
(BBC1 9.15 pm)
Sparky comedy about a struggling Premier League side (could it be Tottenham Hotspur they have in mind?) in the relegation zone near the end of the season. Possible pilot for a series. Watchable.

E

POLIXENES:	We were, fair queen,
	Two lads that thought there was no more behind,
	But such a day tomorrow as today,
	And to be boy eternal.
HERMIONE:	Was not my lord
	The verier wag o' th' two?
POLIXENES:	We were as twinn'd lambs that did frisk i' th' sun,
	And bleat the one at th' other ...

An approach to reading

Effective reading involves several different skills and activities. These are some of the most important.

Defining the task

Start by making sure that you know your aims: **why** are you reading this text?

- for general information?
- to find out a particular fact?
- for fun?
- or what?

Identifying the text

Decide what kind of text you are reading. This will make it easier to understand the text and to achieve your aims. There is more about this in Unit A3.

Finding your way around the text

Try to get a clear picture of how the text is organised and where different kinds of information can be found. There is more about this in Unit A2.

Getting the gist

Now skim the text. Let your eyes run over it quickly to see roughly what it is about. There is more about this in Unit A2.

Understanding the details

Now you can go on to read the text in detail and make sure that you have a thorough understanding of it. There is more about this in Unit A4.

Identifying fact and opinion

You need to be able to distinguish between fact and opinion, especially in non-fiction texts where these two can be confused – for example in newspapers and magazines. There is more about this in Unit A6.

Reading between the lines

With some texts you need to work out meanings that are not stated directly but can be worked out by thinking carefully about what **is** stated. There is more about this in Unit A5.

A2 Finding things

Skimming

When you approach a text it is useful to begin by skimming: letting your eye run over the information and ideas it contains and the way in which they are presented. Look quickly to find out:

- what it is about
- where everything is.

Quick quiz

Look at the text opposite and see how quickly you can find out the answers to these questions:

1 How many paragraphs are there in the text?
2 Most of the text tells a story. How many of the paragraphs are directly concerned with telling that story?
3 These titles could be used to describe the contents of the first three paragraphs. Put them in the right order.

   a Tom begins to die.
   b The hospital diagnoses cancer.
   c Tom becomes ill.

4 Make up similar titles for the remaining paragraphs.
5 These are the key sentences from each of the paragraphs. Put them in the correct order:

   a When Tom was told he was going to die, then he started to die.
   b He did not have cancer at all.
   c The hospital spokesman explained to Tom's wife that the tests had shown a fast-growing cancer.
   d The plain truth is that there is nothing in this world which has such a far-reaching effect on your health as your mind.
   e For several weeks he had a number of persistent and uncomfortable chest symptoms.
   f Within two days Tom had started to deteriorate.

6 Where in the text will you find a reference to each of these? Be careful: some of them appear more than once!

   a witch-doctors
   b a hospital specialist
   c Tom's wife
   d the effects of stress on the body.

Let me start by telling you a story – a true story about a friend of mine called Tom. For several weeks he had a number of persistent and uncomfortable chest symptoms. He had a cough that would not go away and he had some difficulty in getting his breath. The symptoms were quite serious. His doctor tried all the usual drugs, but none of them seemed to work. Although he still managed to get to work, Tom found his symptoms annoying, troublesome and tiring.

Eventually, his family doctor referred him to a specialist at a nearby hospital. The consultant was puzzled but suggested that Tom should spend a few days in hospital so that some tests could be done. After a week, he was sent home. He was no better and no worse, but he had been assured that someone from the hospital would telephone the results of his tests as soon as possible. It was several days before someone rang – and then the news was devastating. The hospital spokesman explained to Tom's wife that the tests had shown a fast-growing cancer. The consultant, it was reported, predicted a rapid decline and death within a month or two.

Within two days Tom had started to deteriorate. The consultant's predictions were coming true. For the first time since the illness began, Tom could not get out of bed. Work became impossible and he felt so weak that he could not eat properly. He began to lose weight and he soon needed constant nursing. Relatives came from all over the country to await the predicted outcome. The house remained quiet, the curtains were drawn and people shuffled around quietly and timidly – talking in whispers.

Then came the second telephone call from the hospital. An apologetic voice told Tom's wife that a mistake had been made. He did not have cancer at all. There had been a mix-up. He had an infection that could be treated with special drugs. Within 24 hours Tom was out of bed and back at work. He could walk and eat again. He still had the chest symptoms, but he was no longer dying.

I have started with this brief but remarkable anecdote because it shows just how powerful the human mind can be. We tend to think of voodoo as a joke. We think it is bizarre that there are people living in Africa or the West Indies who can be so terrified by a threat from a witch-doctor that they will go home and quietly die. Yet the only difference is that our witch-doctors wear white coats and stethoscopes instead of grass skirts and hideous masks. The plain truth is that there is nothing in this world which has such a far-reaching effect on your health as your mind. The way you respond to stress, pressure and worry will determine the condition of your heart, circulatory system, stomach, respiratory system and every other organ and tissue in your body. It is your state of mind which determines what diseases you will develop and how long you will live.

When Tom was told he was going to die, then he started to die. Obediently and politely his mind started to kill his body – fulfilling the prediction made by the doctors. He believed that the doctors knew best and his imagination did the rest. When he was told that there had been a mistake and that he was not going to die, he made an apparently miraculous recovery.

Dr V. Coleman: *Mind over Body*

A3 Same story, different tellers

Looking at how information is presented

Information about the same event can be presented in different ways. Different writers will arrange their ideas in a different order and select different aspects of the subject to emphasise. Even small changes of wording, selection, and order can make a very big difference to the overall message of the text.

These two newspaper reports cover the same story in different ways. Read the two stories which are printed in full on the opposite page and then answer the questions on page 12.

BRAZIL-IANT ... Coulthard

David Coulthard is embraced by one of his McLaren pit crew after his win in Brazil on Sunday.

Coul: I would rather crash than wimp out

DAVID COULTHARD has revealed how he risked having a huge 180mph crash in the blinding rain rather than be labelled an also ran in the Brazilian Grand Prix.

The Scot was roaring down the pit-lane wheel to wheel with Michael Schumacher during the nail-biting showdown when he spotted his chance to zip by the Ferrari star in a torrential downpour and win the race. Coulthard said: 'There's a kink in the straight where you can't see anything, but I knew Michael was on my right.

'At that point you couldn't see a car in front but I refused to back off. I would rather have crashed into someone than trundle round to pick up a place. I could see 10 points in front of me and you don't sit back when the chance of a win is there.

'And this win was brilliant for me. I have never felt so good after a race and I am now right back in the hunt.'

The Sun

Victory brings extra burden for Coulthard

DAVID Coulthard is happy to carry the hopes of his compatriots in Formula 1, but is less comfortable bearing the burden of history. Although the Scot celebrated in traditional fashion after winning Sunday's Brazilian Grand Prix, he was less gung-ho when reminded that every winner of the race since 1993 has gone on to become world champion.

'You know, they had that statistic in Melbourne,' Coulthard said. 'The guy who won Australia went on to win the championship that year.'

But what exactly did he mean? That he paid no heed to supposed precedents? That he could not be relied upon to keep such trends going? Or, more likely, that he would rather live without the pressure of being required to keep a run going for an eighth year?

'There's a long way to go. I'm there in the hunt,' was all the McLaren driver would add when urged to make his meaning clear.

And at least he is right on that count. Coulthard's win at Interlagos ended a sequence of six successive victories for Michael Schumacher's Ferrari, and took the Scot to within six points of his German rival.

After Schumacher had written him off before the race, Coulthard wisely retained his composure and declined to join in a war of words. His caution may well indicate a lack of self-confidence, but it is also a realistic response: you do not get rid of Schumacher's championship challenge by taking a single race.

The victory, nonetheless, was a significant boost for the McLaren-Mercedes-Benz team, who can use it as a springboard to further success, according to Norbert Haug, the head of Mercedes motorsport.

'This is a huge turning point,' Haug said. 'It was about time. We are relieved, but we are careful not to get carried away.

'I am ever so happy for David. He showed what he is really capable of by beating Michael Schumacher in extremely difficult conditions. We have always believed in him, but up to now he did not have the best car.'

The Scotsman

A broad view

1 Both articles describe the same sporting event, and the original information they use is the same. What would you say are the main differences between the two stories?

The data

2 Make a list of the main information contained in both stories. Write as briefly as you can, and use these main headings:

- The sporting event which led to the newspaper report
- Who was involved and why
- The conditions experienced by the drivers in the race
- Why Coulthard's win was so important
- What Coulthard said
- What Haug said.

The approach

3 One report is much longer (only part of the whole story is included). Compare the two stories:

- does the report in *The Sun* miss out any details which you would consider important?
- is the report in *The Scotsman* longer mainly because it contains more information, or for some other reason?

Summing it up

4 Which of the stories is:

- clearer?
- fairer?
- more interesting?

Your writing

5 Both reports show Michael Schumacher in a less flattering light than David Coulthard. Imagine that you are Schumacher's press officer. Immediately after the race you have to make a statement to the press, showing him in a very favourable light, despite his defeat. Write your full press release.

A4 Watch out, there's a granny about

Reading in detail

There are many situations in life where it is important to read carefully and take in all the details of a text – your life may even depend on it. After a first reading to get your bearings, read slowly and make sure that your eye is not skipping important information. If necessary, read some or all of the text more than once.

Read this paragraph carefully and then answer the questions.

Over the last six months, six of my friends in London have been physically assaulted: in all cases without warning and, in every case bar one, by a complete stranger. One girl was left with large chunks of hair torn out and impressive gouges across her face and neck; one man was beaten so hard that he had raised welts across his back under four layers of clothing afterwards. The others escaped with mild shock and bruising. They were all under 30, and they had all been attacked by old age pensioners.

Questions

1 Is each of the following statements true or false?

   a The attacks described average one per week.
   b All the attacks were made by older people on younger people.
   c All the attackers knew their victims.

2 How many of the victims were injured?
3 One of the victims was badly injured on the back. What else do we learn about this person?
4 One girl was attacked. What were her injuries?

Standard Grade English – Credit

Now read the rest of the article and answer the questions at the end.

Natasha, a lawyer, was coming out of a supermarket when an old man turned round and began hitting her with his walking-stick. She ended up having to run away. David had also been hit, repeatedly and very hard, with a walking-stick, after an elderly woman had stepped out in front of his motorbike without waiting for the traffic lights.

15 It was sheer luck, he said, that he didn't kill her; she obviously disagreed. James had been standing, quite innocently, next to a short, pugnacious old man on the tube. He'd begun muttering to himself about the youth of today before suddenly thumping James (28) around the head.

Clare, a BBC director, had brushed against a heavily jewelled, fat old woman at the

20 theatre. 'I apologised,' she said. 'And basically this woman shoved me up against the seat and started punching me.' Much the same thing had happened to Victoria in a cinema. Sarah, unusually, had actually known her attacker, her 75-year-old neighbour. 'You bastard, you bastard,' she was screaming, as she clawed at Sarah's face. 'I'll get you.' They had had a minor disagreement about a door lock a few days earlier; it was

25 the closest any of the attacks came to having a reason.

There's nothing like being assaulted by an OAP to make you start questioning a few basic assumptions about old people. Judging by newspaper headlines, pensioners exist to provide the youth of today with slow-moving targets, not the other way round. Last Monday, the newspapers all seemed to carry the same photograph of

30 36-year-old WPC Lynn Butler, dressed and made up to look like a helpless old granny. The idea is that her male colleagues in Birmingham hid round a corner waiting for WPC Butler to be attacked by young muggers whom they then arrest.

Old people have a clearly defined role as society's victims; over the years, poster campaigns showing white-haired old ladies gazing mournfully at the outside world

35 have drummed home the same message. The old are vulnerable. The old are innocent. Old people need your help. Be nice to them. Despite the Government's efforts the old have continued to be victims. According to a recent survey, one in 20 old people is estimated to suffer from some form of abuse. The Government, which has obviously given up trying to persuade people to be nice to the old, is starting

40 telephone helplines for the abused elderly instead. In October, guilt will be piled upon guilt, as the calls come in and the age-related charities wearily repeat the message that pensioners are nice people with a lot to offer society, if only society would get round to realising it.

The fact that I know half a dozen people who have been assaulted by pensioners (and

45 no one who has been assaulted by anyone else) should be shocking. But the assumption that old people are invariably victims is, in any case, becoming increasingly untenable. Thanks to medical advances, the NHS and private pension schemes, pensioners today bear little resemblance to the pensioners of 50 years ago. Over two-thirds of them now draw on occupational pensions, instead of having to rely

50 on the state. Pensioners make up around one-sixth of Britain's population but now get 40 per cent of the £22 billion spent annually on hospitals and community health care services. For every house-bound, poverty-stricken old lady, there are increasing numbers of fit, comfortably-off, pensionable house-owners more likely to be booking Saga holidays than signing for meals-on-wheels.

Few people of my age can understand why we should always forgive old people's rudeness, their intolerance, their apparently miraculous ability to be hobbling down a street one minute and galloping towards a free bus seat with the speed of a turbo-charged Zimmer frame the next. Legally, they get to play by an entirely different set of rules, as Sarah, the one person who reported being attacked by an OAP, found out. The police, who hardly smirked at all, agreed she had a case, but advised her to drop it. 'Let's face it, love,' they told her, 'no court's going to convict an old granny, no matter what she's done.' Just because there are only a handful of pensioners currently in prison does not mean that more don't deserve to be. 'In all seriousness,' agreed a Police Federation spokesman, 'we could be looking at a real problem here. If old people think they can get away with it, we're in danger of sending the wrong message.'

Publicly, people rarely challenge the idea that old people deserve their special status, an automatic right to bad behaviour, even their freedom to drive atrociously without ever having to take a driving test. Privately, quite a few people are obviously starting to wonder why. If pensioners are fit enough to beat up a 27-year-old, they are fit enough to be made to do community service. The excuse that the pensioners of today are the war heroes of yesterday no longer washes: people who are 65 now were too young then to do any more than keep the home fires burning. No matter how you look at it, it doesn't make sense that old people should continue to be either rewarded or pitied for being old. They are lucky to be old. The alternative is being dead.

The Spectator

Questions

Lines 11–18

5 Copy and complete this table:

	Natasha	David	James	✔ = Yes
Attacker elderly?	✔	✔	✔	✘ = No
Attack violent?				
Weapon used?				
Unprovoked?				

6 Use the table to explain what all these attacks had in common.

Lines 19–25

7 Make up a similar table for this paragraph to the one in question 5.

8 What do these attacks have in common?

Lines 26–32

9 What 'basic assumptions about old people' does this paragraph describe?

Lines 33–43

10 What is meant by the words, 'Old people have a clearly defined role as society's victims'?

11 What aspects of being a 'victim' does the writer list?

12 What does the writer say about the Government's attitude to this?

Lines 44–54

13 Make a list of the ways in which the writer says that the situation of old people has changed in the past fifty years.

14 How would you sum up the effects of these changes?

Lines 55–66

15 The writer gives a number of reasons for criticising old people. What are they?

16 What was the attitude of the police to the attack on Sarah and what were their views on the wider problem of violence by old people?

Lines 67–76

17 What is the contrast the writer remarks on between what people say 'publicly' and think 'privately'?

18 Why does the writer say that old people 'are lucky to be old'?

The whole argument

Look back over the answers you have given to questions 1–18. Use them to help you answer these broad questions about the whole argument.

19 What are the incidents that have led the writer to express these views about old people?

20 What is the traditional view of old people that the writer describes?

21 Why does the writer consider that such a view is out of date?

22 How would you sum up the writer's attitude to old people?

A5 *I know what it says, but what does it mean?*

Reading 'between the lines'

Reading is an active process. You don't just sit there letting the words go into your head; your mind is active. You ask yourself questions about the text and use your intelligence and imagination to try to work out the answers. Using the evidence in front of you, you guess:

- what is 'behind' the words on the page
- in a story, what has happened before and what will happen next
- in a poem, what is deliberately being left unsaid.

We have to work particularly hard when we read the opening of a story:

'Dad? Dad! It's Eve.
How are you? What are you doing with yourself? Are you all right?'
'Eve? Eve darling, how are you? God, it's good to hear your voice. Where are you? ...

It's a daughter talking to her father.

They haven't seen each other for some time.

They aren't in the same place, so they must be talking by phone or radio.

What can you work out from the next few sentences of the story?

... Why can't I see you?'
Eve smiled happily. It was so good to hear if not see her Dad again. Somehow it made the idea of returning home seem closer and more real. 'Dad, the screen of this video-phone isn't working. And the fleet's just returned to Tdir-ah so the queues to use the phones are *ginormous*. It was use this phone or wait for another week to find a phone with a working screen.'
'No, no, it's enough just hearing your voice, bunny. Are you all right?'
'I'm fine Dad.' Eve smiled again, stretching out a tentative arm to the blank screen before her. 'I've missed you so much. I just can't wait to get home.'
'So the reports are true? The war *is* finally over?'

Malorie Blackman: *Not so Stupid!*

Now see what you can understand from this story opening. There are some prompt questions beside it to guide your thoughts.

The journey to Pitmedden had always been longer than the journey back. But this time it seemed even longer, as if Pitmedden had become further from Edinburgh than ever before.

It was only on my mother's insistence, and with an ill grace, that my
5   father had allowed me to go with them this time, and he started making up for it as soon as we were on the road. He was in a touchy mood, of course, after being taken down a peg by my mother, and his voice was sharper than usual as he laid down the law on what I could do and what I should not do when we reached my grandfather's smallholding.
10 'This is a sick visit, not a holiday. You'll not get up to any mischief with Willie Webster and his like. You've your new school uniform on, remember, and you'll keep it clean and do nothing to disgrace it. Are you listening?'

'Ye-es,' I drawled with a hint of defiance.
15 My mother turned round and gave me one of her looks – the look that pleaded with me not to provoke him. Although she had spoken against him when he had argued that I should stay in Edinburgh with my aunt, she sided with him in most things. She was always trying to persuade me that he was strict with me only because he wanted me
20 to follow his example and get on in the world. 'He's come a long way since he ran barefoot in Pitmedden,' she often said. 'We have to keep up with him. We're Pitmedden folk, and Pitmedden folk hang together.' Hunched in the back seat of the new car, our first car, I stared sullenly at his balding head. It was the only bare part of him now.
25 Rain fell in torrents from the low clouds darkening the sky. We were travelling in midwinter, only a few days before Christmas, and the countryside I knew so well in the green and gold of summer was now hardly recognisable, stripped to its dark skin, wet bone. Rain and resentment made a misery out of what had always before been the
30 happiest of journeys for me – a journey that had seemed long only because of my impatience to reach Pitmedden and a freedom I could never find in Edinburgh. Nothing raised my spirits until my father lost his way.

'We must have taken the wrong turning at the last junction,' he said coolly, as if we were all to blame.
35 My mother's impatience got the better of her. 'We should have gone by the train as usual.'

I knew better than to say anything, but I watched him with a spiteful pleasure as he turned the car and headed back towards the junction. It was not often I had the chance to see him taken down two pegs in
40 one day.

James Allan Ford: *Pitmedden Folk*

- Where is the story set?

- Why are they making the journey?

- What reasons might there be for the father's mood?

- What can you say about the relationship between the boy and his father?

- What is the significance of the mother giving *one of her looks?*

- What can you conclude about the father's childhood?

- How does the setting influence the mood?

- Why is the boy's pleasure *spiteful?*

- Will things on the journey get better or worse?

- What might happen next?

Poems often depend on our curiosity and willingness to read between the lines to say a lot in a small space. Read this poem and use the prompt questions alongside to help you work out what is going on.

This Year

1

As the days grew shorter we'd sing our way home
                                    through the darkness
– your voice in front, mine half a beat behind.
Trees clawed at us and the wind hissed
– I held your coat tight.

2

This year we keep to the concrete path round the building.
Tea and biscuits in your room. A bed, a chair, radio,
some photographs – you say you've everything you need.

Another day has passed, another evening. I'll leave soon.
I have to. When the trees press too close our hands touch:

There is no singing, no road home.

Ron Butlin

- Who is the speaker?
- Who is being spoken to?
- How do the words *clawed* and *hissed* contribute to the atmosphere being created?

- What differences are implied by the contrast between *building* (line 5) and *home* (line 1)?
- What does line 9 tell you about the mood of the speaker?
- Why do you think the writer has chosen to mention these two things in the closing line?

Writing

The poem gives us a snapshot of a relationship between people of different ages. Write a paragraph describing the picture you have formed in your mind of the relationship between them in verse 1.

Now write another paragraph describing how their relationship has changed over time, as described in verse 2.

A6 Is that a fact?

Fact and opinion

When reading non-fiction it is often important to distinguish between facts and opinions.

A **fact** is a statement that can be shown to be true. For example:

Edinburgh is the capital city of Scotland.

An **opinion** is an expression of a personal belief. For example:

Glasgow has a better shopping centre than Edinburgh.

You cannot prove that Glasgow is better in such a way that everyone will agree with you; different people will have different views.

Which is which?

Divide these statements into three groups:

- fact
- opinion
- a mixture of fact and opinion.

1 The only ice-cream worth eating is chocolate chip.
2 Islamabad is the capital of Pakistan.
3 Rover make cars, but not as well as Renault.
4 Linford Christie is one of the all-time greats of British athletics.
5 Henry VIII who ruled in the sixteenth century was married several times.
6 If you want a good time, spend a weekend in Wigan.

What the papers say

Newspapers contain a mixture of fact and opinion. Often they don't agree in their interpretation of the news. Here are two headlines and photographs from the day when a famous tennis player lost a valuable sponsorship contract:

Steffi, laughing off a $1m loss

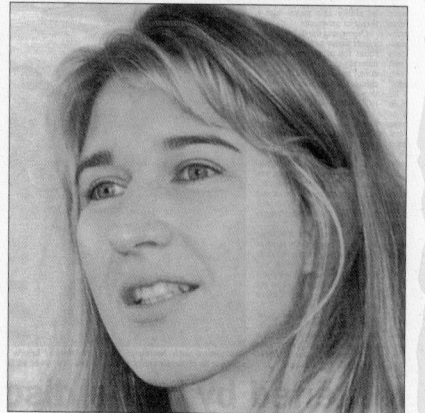

Desolate Graf talks of ordeal

The Independent, 17 October 1995

'Fact is sacred'

Traditionally the 'news' pages contain facts and the 'opinion' columns contain opinions.

Fact

Shots were fired at the motorcade of Bangladesh's main opposition leader yesterday, a day after a bomb at a governing party rally
5 killed at least 22 people. Khaleda Zia, the leader of the Bangladesh Nationalist Party, was unhurt after two bullets hit a van carrying security guards just behind her
10 vehicle. She accused the government of trying to kill her. Zia's party said members of the governing Awami League stopped the motorcade 20 miles south of
15 Dhaka during a trip to give speeches in southern Bangladesh. The two sides grew violent after Zia's supporters tried to remove logs and scrap iron blocking the road.

The Herald

Opinion

The BBC is secretly considering selling off its transmitters. Not interested? You should be. It is the transmitters that bring pro-
5 grammes into your home. Consider what would happen if they ended up in the hands of a private company out to make money for its bosses and share-
10 holders. Transmitters PLC could be an incredibly powerful mono-poly. What would happen if it decided to land the BBC with a huge bill for its services? Would
15 the BBC find the money by cutting the amount of cash it puts into making programmes? Or would it find some way of increasing the licence fee? In short, do you trust
20 fat cats to control your viewing? Quite. And neither do we.

The Daily Mirror

Quite often, however, popular newspapers combine fact and opinion and present it as 'news':

Blast for teachers

OPINION → Loudmouth Leftie teachers who mobbed
FACT → blind MP David Blunkett are off the hook.
OPINION → The rabble-rousers will not be punished
5 and are back in the classroom, it was → FACT
revealed yesterday. → FACT
And they haven't even apologised for
OPINION → their brutal actions at the NUT conference in Blackpool last month.
10 Angry Mr Blunkett, Labour's education spokesman, said: 'How can they command respect in the classroom now and undo the damage they've done their profession?' → It's a FACT that he said it, but he's expressing his OPINION

The Star

1 Read each of these three newspaper cuttings carefully.
2 Decide whether each cutting is mainly fact, mainly opinion, or a mixture of the two.
3 If you decide that a cutting is a mixture, find examples in it of both fact and opinion to prove your point.

Refs: Only players can stop the dives

Scottish football's referees supremo Donald McVicar has appealed to top players to take it upon themselves to end the recent upsurge in play-acting incidents.

5   Damaging television pictures suggested that Paul Lambert grossly exaggerated the effect of an Ian Ferguson challenge to gain a crucial penalty in Celtic's victory over Dunfermline on Monday night.

10   The Scotland midfielder last night maintained a diplomatic silence in the face of questioning from his closest colleagues. However former Grade One referee McVicar has again ruled out the possibility

15 of using greater television evidence to aid referees on such occasions.

The Park Gardens official said: 'Diving, or simulation as it is also known, is effectively the act of players deceiving

20 fellow professionals and the supporters for their own gain and perhaps it's time it was discussed in another forum.

'We have consistently pointed to the issues involved in cheating, but the ultimate

25 responsibility falls on the players to have a good look at themselves.

'We can only do so much and we will do what we can to stamp on it, but the only solution may be self-regulation amongst

30 those who play the game professionally.

'We already use video evidence to some extent but it will never be used to change the results of matches or alter refereeing decisions. It may be used in cases of

35 mistaken identity but I cannot foresee any real changes.'

The Daily Mail

Still smiling aged 120

FRENCHWOMAN Jeanne Calment, who once met Vincent Van Gogh, is certain to be smiling tomorrow – she will become the oldest person who ever lived, aged 120 years

5 and 238 days. *The Guinness Book of Records* lists Shigechiyo Izumi of Japan, who died in 1986 at 120 years and 237 days, as the current record holder. 'Always keep your smile,' said Jeanne, who is confined to a wheelchair at a

10 nursing home in Arles. 'That's how I explain my long life. I think I will die laughing.'

The Daily Express

We send in the girls

Tears and pride as women soldiers join lads in Bosnia battle zone hell

Three brave Army girls were last night helping to spearhead the massive airlift to save Our Boys in Bosnia.

Lance-Corporal Susan Taylor and Signaller

5 Tracy Farr boarded a Hercules yesterday to fly out with a squad of male comrades.

And Corporal Tracey Duggan was on standby waiting to join them with her own unit, the fearsome 24 Air-mobile Brigade.

10 Susan, 21, and Tracy, 24, both of 30 Signals, left RAF Lyneham in Wiltshire for the Croatian port of Split.

For blonde Tracy the order to go brought joy – for it will reunite her with her soldier boyfriend.

15 Corporal John Poole, 27, who is also in 30 Signals, was flown out with an earlier detachment five weeks ago. The couple began dating when Tracy returned to Britain from a year-long stint in Wildenrath, Germany.

20 They vowed to wait for each other when John was sent off with an advance party of the regiment, based in Nuneaton, Warwicks.

The Sun

A7 Approaching writing

Who? What? Why?

Before we start writing, we need to have a clear idea of:

- who we are writing for
- what we are writing
- why we are writing.

Writing to **communicate**

Writing for ourselves

Writing to **remember**

See unit A11

Writing to **understand**

See unit A12

Writing for others

Why?

- to inform
- to persuade
- to regulate
- to interact
- to entertain
- to record

See unit A8

Who?

- What do they know?
- What do they understand?
- How well do I know them?

See units A9, A10

How?

You may find it helpful to use this plan before and during any piece of writing you do.

Defining the task

You should have a clear idea of:

- the kind of writing you are going to do
- the audience it is intended for
- the purpose of your writing.

If you are unsure of these points your writing will not be clear or effective.

Before moving on, ask yourself, 'Am I satisfied with this?'

If the answer is 'No', go back and do some more work on **Defining the task**

If the answer is 'Yes', go on to **Preparing**

Preparing

This involves:

- generating ideas (either alone, or with others)
- researching information.

Before moving on, ask yourself, 'Am I satisfied with this?'

If the answer is 'No', go back and do some more work on **Preparing**

If the answer is 'Yes', go on to **Planning**

Planning

You need to plan:

- the key points you want to make
- the order in which you want to make them.

Sometimes you can plan in your head. Often it is a good idea to make some notes on paper, especially if the topic is at all complicated.

Before moving on, ask yourself, 'Am I satisfied with this?'

If the answer is 'No', go back and do some more work on **Planning**

If the answer is 'Yes', go on to **Drafting**

Drafting

You may write one or more **drafts**:

1 Write the first version of your text.
2 If possible, get someone else to read it and comment on it. A good method is to work with a partner, or in a small group, so that you can share the task of reading and commenting on each other's writing. Otherwise, read your own writing and imagine that you are another reader.
3 When you write a second draft, change those sections of the text that were unsatisfactory and fill any gaps you have noticed.

Editing

When you read a draft through and think about it, you are editing.
Ask yourself:

- Have I included all the ideas and information needed?
- Is it all in the best order?
- Have I expressed it as well as I can?

Depending on your answers to these questions, you may need to make changes, or write a further draft.

Before moving on, ask yourself, 'Am I satisfied with this?'

If the answer is 'No', go back and do some more work on **Editing**	If the answer is 'Yes', go on to **Proof reading**

Proof reading

You then need to check for mistakes of:

- grammar
- punctuation
- spelling.

Presentation

Now you need to prepare your work for others to read. Think about who will read it and the form in which they will see it. Think of the best way to:

- present the text (handwriting, word-processing?)
- make the layout clear
- use headings.

Warning

The stages have been presented as if you always had plenty of time and could take them one at a time. Sometimes you can't – in a timed examination, for example. In those cases you may have to combine stages. For example, there may only be time to write one draft. You will then have to edit as you write and make any alterations needed as neatly as possible. However, all writing for an audience goes through all the stages described here.

A8 Why write?

Purposes for writing

Whenever we write we have one or more purposes. The commonest of these are:

- to inform
- to persuade
- to regulate (to tell someone else what to do)
- to interact (to 'get on with someone else' – for example, a personal letter)
- to entertain
- to record (for example, a diary).

Look at these texts and then answer the questions that follow them.

A

Cut a dash to FRANCE

Step out in style this summer aboard the elegant SeaCat. It's in a class of its own as it glides effortlessly between Folkestone and Boulogne in just 55 minutes.

The twin hulled catamaran's striking good looks are perfectly complemented with a tastefully appointed interior. Relax in the spacious and modern surroundings, ordering drinks and duty free goods from the comfort of your seat – or take in the air on the outer deck.

B

REMEMBER: if you sell or pass this vehicle to someone else

- You must fill in the 'notification of Sale or Transfer' slip overleaf and send it to DVLC yourself to show that you are no longer responsible for this vehicle or its use.

C

Ávila is the highest city in Spain – it is also one of the country's most enchanting, a medieval walled town of great presence. If you arrive at dusk, the walls are softly illuminated. Built of dark granite in the last decade of the 11th century, they stretch for some two-and-a-half kilometres, crenellated and enclosing Ávila in a powerful stone rectangle, 12 metres high and three metres thick.

D

7.00	Top of the Pops (T) (S) *7035*
7.30	EastEnders (T) (S) *734*
8.00	Zoo Watch Live (T) (S) *6783*
8.30	Agony Again (T) (S) *5290*

E

A great scandal of the modern NHS

There is one person without whose input my entire NHS practice would grind to a halt. The management of all my patients with cancer, and the less serious conditions, is utterly dependent on her reliability and competence. I refer, of course, to my secretary. The fact that she is paid less than the secretary of one of the hospital managers is one of the greatest scandals of the modern NHS. It is high time that the invaluable contribution of these essential employees is recognised, and that their salaries reflect their crucial role in the deliverance of modern healthcare.

A. Lawrie Morton
Consultant Urologist
Royal Alexandra Hospital, Paisley

from *The Herald*

F

Most of my childhood was spent in a women-only world. Five of us; my mother, grandmother, two aunts and myself lived in a room and kitchen on the ground floor of a tenement in Glasgow's East End. We shared two hole-in-the-wall beds. Three of us slept in the four-foot-wide one in the kitchen, two in the two-foot-six one in the 'room'. In spite of a pervading emphasis on modesty, there was little privacy to be found except by going to the outside lavatory at the back of the close.

Kay Carmichael: *Dreams in Cold Storage*

Analysing the texts

Think about the answers to these questions:

1 What is each text about?
2 Where does it come from?
3 What kind of person might it be aimed at?

Copy and complete this table:

Text	Topic	Source	Purpose(s)	Comments on language
A	cross-channel catamaran services	advertisement in newspaper or magazine	to inform to persuade	1: uses several commands ('Cut a dash'; 'Step out in style'). This gives it a sense of urgency. 2: uses very positive and persuasive words ('elegant', 'glides', 'effortlessly')

Republic of Dominica

NATIONAL PROFILE

Hispaniola, the island shared by Haiti and the Dominican Republic, was Columbus' first stopover in the New World. Since 1492 it has changed hands several times, with the Spanish, Americans and French playing a part. Even Sir Francis Drake and Nelson had designs on the island. Major figures include Toussaint l'Ouverture, who led a slave revolt in the 1790s; Duarte, who led the struggle for independence from Haiti in 1844; and Trujillo, the dictator who seized power in 1930. Since the 1960s there has been a relatively stable democratic government. The president, Joaquin Balaguer, 88 and blind, was returned to office in 1994. Malpractice was suspected on all sides.

CLIMATE

It's always warm, reaching 40°C/104°F in August. The rainy season is May to September, with a risk of hurricanes from August to October. There are short downpours from November to January.

SIGHTS/EXCURSIONS

Take a trip to Lake Enriquillo, 44 m below sea level, to see the iguanas, flamingos and crocodiles on Isla Cabritos in the centre. There are whale-watching trips from the Semaná peninsula from December to March.

LANGUAGE

Spanish is the official language. Some English and German is spoken.

FOOD AND DRINK

In bars, expect to pay £1 for a sandwich, 90p for a beer, and 50p for a Coke. In local shops, expect to pay £4 for a bottle of cheap plonk, and 70p for a litre of water. The main options for vegetarians are rice, beans and fruit.

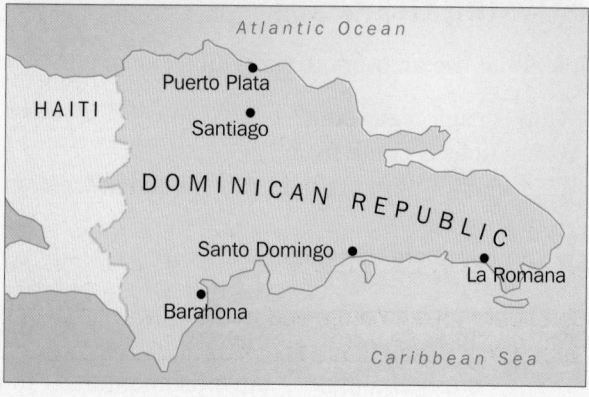

BBC *Holidays*

What to do

1   Read the text carefully.
2   Use the information it contains to write both assignments.

Assignments

■ The text for the introduction to a travel brochure offering holidays in the Dominican Republic.

■ An entry for an illustrated information book about the Caribbean, written for 6–8-year-olds.

A9 Who's it for?

Thinking of your audience

It's no use writing for someone else if they find your writing difficult or impossible to understand. So writers have to think of the needs of their audience. They have to consider:

- how well they can use English
  This may be a question of age, education, or whether English is their first language or not.
- how well they can read
  Again this will depend on age, education, and mother tongue.
- how much they know about the subject.

Words

Some words are easier to read and understand than others. If a piece of writing contains too many hard words it will be difficult to understand. Divide the following list of words into three groups.

A words that could be read and understood by a child of seven.
B words that you can read and understand, but which don't belong in Group **A.**
C words that you would need help in understanding.

bilge	castoff	clinker	debris	dross	flotsam	jetsam	jumble
junk	litter	lumber	refuse	rejects	rubbish	spoilage	trash

When you are writing for a particular audience, it is important to use words that they can be expected to know.

Sentences

The way in which sentences are written can also make a text easier or harder to read. Put these three extracts in order, with the easiest first and the hardest last.

A The public is encouraged to separate paper and glass for recycling and to avoid throwing away high-hazard items with the domestic waste.

B Sort your rubbish before you throw it away. Collect paper and glass for recycling. Do not throw dangerous things away with ordinary rubbish.

C People should collect paper and glass for recycling and should not throw away dangerous things with household rubbish.

Why have you placed them in that order?

Think about:

- vocabulary
- how long the sentences are
- how complicated the sentences are
- the punctuation.

Reading about rubbish

Read these two texts and then answer the questions below:

A

> Not all of our rubbish needs to be thrown away. Some of it can be used again – like the empty milk bottles people put on the doorstep each day.
>
> Some of our rubbish can't be used again, but it can help to make new materials. This is called recycling.
>
> Do you know of any materials that can be recycled?

Nigel Hawkes: *Toxic Waste and Recycling*

B

> The industrial world is also realising that many waste materials are too valuable to throw away. Old cars are 'cannibalised' for spare parts in scrap yards, then melted down as scrap which goes to make steel for another generation of cars. Some glass bottles can be used up to thirty times if they are collected and cleaned. Broken glass – 'cullet' – can be recycled to make new bottles, saving raw materials and energy. Waste paper can also be used again. In 1984, paper recycling programmes in nine industrial countries spared a million acres of trees. Recycling aluminium drink cans requires only a twentieth as much energy as making fresh aluminium from bauxite ore.

Claire Llewellyn: *Rubbish*

Questions

Both these extracts come from information books written for children aged 5–11.

1 List any difficult words in extract **A**
2 List the difficult words in extract **B**
3 Are there any difficult sentences in **A**?
4 Are there any in **B**?
5 What age group would extract **A** be suitable for?
6 What age group would extract **B** be suitable for?

Writing

1 Read extract **B** carefully, making sure that you understand it!
2 Make a list of the main ideas and information it contains.
3 Re-write it so that it is suitable for the readers of extract **A**.
4 Compare the two versions. How much detailed information have you had to leave out?

Knowledge level

It is also important to be aware of what your readers know about the subject already and what they don't know. Read this text and then follow the instructions.

If you are in Northern France during the third week of June, driving west of Paris, you will be overtaken by a steady stream of unlikely vehicles: overladen Peugeots, priceless Lamborghinis, home-made plastic kit-cars and ancient camper vans tottering under the weight of too many tents.

All will be full of happy grinning faces in holiday mood and will be driven just about as fast as they can go. They are on an annual pilgrimage to the Lourdes of motor racing: Le Mans.

Until 1923 Le Mans was just an uninspiring industrial town in north-west France. Then the local motor-club decided to run a car race on a 13 km triangle of public roads just outside the town. To make sure the world took notice, they made it a race that would go on all day and all night.

Les Vingt-Quatre Heures du Mans was born [20] and the name of Le Mans went for ever into the motor-racing lexicon. This year's will be the 63rd and over 150,000 people will converge on the town for the occasion.

I will be one of them. All my life I have been [25] entranced by the romance of this round-the-clock race. As a small boy at prep-school in the 1950s I used to smuggle a radio into the dormitory to listen to the BBC reports under the bedclothes, with Raymond Baxter's [30] educated tones describing the Jaguar v Ferrari battles through the night.

BBC *Worldwide* magazine

What to do

Your own knowledge

1 Make a list of any words or phrases in the text that you are not familiar with.
2 List any other questions that the text raises which you cannot answer.
3 Try to find out the meanings of unknown words and the answers to your other questions.

The text and the reader

4 Now look through the text again and list any other technical terms and pieces of background knowledge that the writer assumes the reader will understand. Against each one, write comments like this:

Item	Comments
'Lourdes'	The reader needs to know it is a place of pilgrimage for Roman Catholics

Your writing

5 Write two short descriptions of one of these topics:

- for a reader who is familiar with Scotland
- for an overseas reader who speaks English well, but has never visited this country.

Topics

- the Scottish school system
- a Scottish inn
- your favourite television programme.

A10 *It depends if I know them or not*

Tone and formality

The way in which we address other people – in speech or writing – is called **tone**. It is made up of:

- the words we use
- the way in which we construct our sentences
- (if we are speaking) the way in which we pronounce words and sentences.

If we are addressing someone we do not know we are more likely to use more **formal** language. With friends we are more likely to be **informal**. On the other hand, there are situations when we may want to be formal with a person we know well – for example, two teachers who are friends will talk to each other differently if they are in front of a class than when they are alone together.

You can place people and situations – and the language they produce – on a diagram like this:

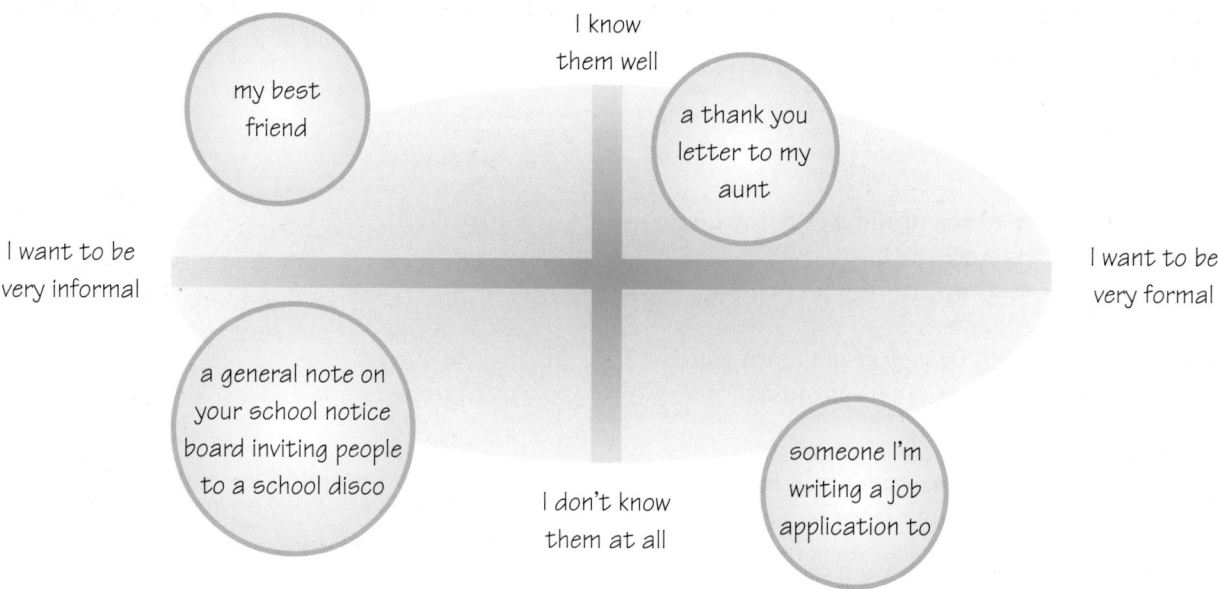

In other words:

- you know your best friend very well and speak very informally to him or her
- when you apply for a job you are writing to someone you have never met and you want to be fairly formal
- you know your aunt fairly well and want to write a formal thank you letter which is also friendly
- you may not know the people who respond to your note on the noticeboard but you want it to be informal.

Using the diagram

1 Make a copy of the diagram. Place each of these people on it:

- your English teacher
- your brother or sister.

Now think of other people and place them on the diagram.

2 Where would you place each of these greetings on the diagram?

Hi!	All right?	Long time no see.
How do you do?	How's tricks?	Look what the cat's brought in.
How're you doing?	Hallo.	Good morning.

Situations

Match report

You have been asked to write two short reports on a school sports match:

1 in a letter to a close friend, who is very interested but who has been away from school because they are ill
2 to be read out in a school/house/tutor group meeting shortly after the event.

Write the two short texts.

Where would you place each of these two writing situations on the diagram?

Damage limitation

The background

There has been a great deal of damage to furniture and fittings in your school recently. Much of it was unintentional, caused by accidents or people messing around, rather than vandalism. Attitudes towards it vary:

You and your friends:
It's just one of those things that happen.

Your register teacher:
It's understandable, with great awkward people like you lot, but something's got to be done about it.

The head teacher:
The school budget is already tight and you cannot afford to go on having repair bills this big. On the other hand you don't want to make a big fuss about it – there are more important things in life.

The Chair of the School Board:
It's a disgrace and the school's reputation will suffer – it will get a name for being a home for vandals.

What happened

You and a friend were having an argument. Your friend over-reacted and threw a heavy bag full of books at you. You ducked and the bag smashed a large window. Later the damage was discovered by the register teacher, who reported it to the head teacher. They have now said that unless the person who did it owns up, the whole class will have to share the cost (about £50). The Chair of the School Board has heard about it and telephoned the head teacher to demand action.

Write

1 A letter from you to a friend who has recently left the school and moved away, describing what happened.
2 A letter from the head teacher to the Chair of the School Board, explaining what happened and how the culprits have owned up.

Decide where each of these would come on the diagram you have been using. Think carefully about the language and tone that would be suitable for each letter.

A11 Make it snappy!

Making notes

An important way we use writing in school is to help us remember things, by making notes. As with any other kind of writing, one of the most important questions to ask yourself is: 'Who is going to have to read my notes?'

1 If they are just for your own use, then there are only two rules:

  - make your notes as short as possible
  - make sure that you can understand them later.

2 If you are writing for someone else, then you have to think about whether they will be able to understand what you have written.

3 If you are writing notes for a particular subject teacher, then you will probably be told how the notes should be presented.

Specific heat capacity test.

15 June

We did this simple experiment to find out the specific heat capacity of different materials. This is what we used:

Equipment.

Matt,
Thermometer,
Heating eliment,
power pack (50 watt),
1k of : Al,
Cu,
Fe,
Brass,
H2O,

Small quantity of oil.

The masses of metal and thermometers set...

coursework 18 marks.
How does the quality of the housing enviroment vary from one part of the urban area to another.
- do not produce a purely descriptive work
- this is an investigation - answering questions - election distance of Housing density

Wayne Davies

the report - density
A - Paragraph
table (street etc)
- aims
going to investigate?

Joint Rule
1980 anglo-irish summit - wasp discussed
1985 Anglo-Irish agreement - Hillsbough agreement. Regular meeting to discuss cross border relations.
Unionists didn't like it
I.R.A. also objected to 'sell out'/give up'.

Withdraw troops.

loads of weapons in Ireland - could be used in a civil war. Figures more troops the more deaths is Maybe would they withdrew troops & war would start.

Full intergration with the Republic.

Womens peace movement 1976 by Betty Williams & Mairead Corrigan 1977 nobel peace prize.

Joint schooling - A slow process. Theatre groups do plays from both sides.

Investment is Job creation.

Punishment Shootings. Do it to there own side for mixing with other side '89 16, punishment shootings 96 by Republicans 65 by loyalists.

Notes on Solutions

Northan Ireland Parlement Stormont - failed to cope ended 1972.

Northan Ireland Assembly, 1982 Part of "rolling Devpltution" slow to return to self government. SDLP refused to join Unionists left in 1983 after bombing of protestant church.

Direct Rule Imposed in 1972. is it working.

Research

Think back over the past few days. How many times have you made notes?

1 For what school subjects did you do this?
2 On what other occasions in school did you make notes?
3 On what occasions outside school?
4 What are the differences between making notes and writing in full?

Advice on making notes

- pick out key words that sum up whole sentences
- cut out little words like a, an, the, and (use + instead)
- use lines, arrows and other visual guides when you can
- use different colours to highlight important words or sections
- take plenty of space.

High technology medicine

Twentieth-century developments in science and technology have strongly influenced **medicine**. In 1914 scientists had identified the **germs** that cause some diseases, but almost all the **drugs** doctors used were ancient remedies. No one knew how they worked or was sure if they worked at all. But the scientists were

5 already looking for drugs that could kill germs inside the body. In the 1920s and 1930s they began to find them, and since then have found many others which can deal with most infectious diseases. **Penicillin** is probably the most important of these, since it can kill a wide range of germs. It came into use in 1943 after a crash wartime programme of development in Britain and the USA.

10 The new drugs like penicillin greatly helped the surgeon by making operations safer. So did the **blood transfusion system**, developed before and during the First World War. At about the same time, **X-rays** came into use. Like the more recent ultrasound scanners, they enable doctors to see what is wrong inside the body. Other machines such as **heart-lung machines** can take over for a time the work of

15 human organs. By the 1960s surgeons using such high-technology methods could replace a damaged organ with a healthy one taken from an accident victim.

Joe Scott: *The World since 1914*

High-tech medicine
Influenced by 20th C science and technology:

DRUGS	OTHER DEVELOPMENTS
1914 Had identified germs causing disease	1910 → Development of:
BUT drugs still unscientific	blood transfusion system
1920s ⎫ Discovery of drugs that would	medical use of X-rays
1930s ⎭ cure disease inside the body	
1943 PENICILLIN first used	

Surgical operations made much safer
1960s Human transplant surgery possible

Experiment

Now do this experiment to see how well you can make notes.
Follow the instructions exactly.

1 Read the text below and make notes on it. Allow only ten minutes.
2 When the ten minutes are up, close the book.
3 Use your notes to retell the story in as much detail as you can.
4 Open the book again and check your version against the original.
5 Underneath your version, write down any important details you have
  missed out.

Dummy runs that end in death

A mystery man found at the edge of a road by a passing motorist, after
being struck by a hit-and-run driver, was taken to an intensive care
unit in Glasgow.

Paramedics and accident and emergency staff inserted a chest drain
5 and a breathing tube. As the man lay unconscious in intensive care, his
body covered in bruises, abnormal chest and heart sounds were
detected. X-rays revealed eight fractured ribs; other tests that blood
sugar levels were high.

He was put on a ventilator, and lines to monitor blood pressure and
10 feed fluids and drugs were inserted. For the next five days, he was
tended by more than 40 people. Always in a coma, his condition
fluctuated.

His carers knew him only as George, and that he was 22: bare facts
gleaned from rifling his pockets, after debating the ethics of doing so.
15 Despite their best efforts, George died (yet again) late on Friday. His
carers had included student nurses Allan Reid and Julie Thirde, who
are even younger than their patient.

The 21-year-olds had to break the news to George's parents and
girlfriend, who somehow had tracked him down. Just as they will do
20 so soon – in the real world of hospitals.

Because George is a mannequin who lies in a simulated intensive
care unit at Glasgow Caledonian University. He can wheeze, even
have a cardiac arrest, on demand – and, unknown to the students, was
doomed from the start: killed, week in, week out, by lecturers as part
25 of their education process.

The Herald

A12 What's going on here?

Writing to understand

Writing can help us to think more clearly:

- we can use it to help us to speculate, to think around a subject and develop our ideas
- we can use it to force ourselves to clarify our thought, by paraphrasing.

Speculating

When you are working on something that is complicated or puzzling, it is very useful to jot down your ideas on paper, as you think things through.

Paraphrasing

When you are beginning to understand something, it is a useful exercise to write down what you think it means, using complete sentences. This will soon show you those parts of the subject you do understand and those you don't.

Sometimes a writer will present a story in a way that seems mystifying. It can be useful to jot down thoughts and ideas as you read and try to work out what is going on:

Text	Notes
I had seen the collision coming, but when it happened the impact was so abrupt and stunning that it shocked the sense out of me, and for a while I sat quietly among the broken glass	collision – between what and what?
5 of the jeep as though I had been sitting there forever. In any case I found I could not move because of the dead weight of the soldiers on either side of me. We had hit the bus head-on.	jeep – wartime? Which war?
The front of the jeep was embedded under its	soldiers – war?
10 bonnet, and the crash must have somehow distorted the wiring apparatus because the first thing I became aware of was a continuous metallic howl from the horn that nobody tried to stop. It seemed as though the machinery itself	bus – can't really be a war if there's a bus full of people. Perhaps a <u>civil</u> war?
15 was screaming in pain, while all the people involved were spellbound and silent.	Why are all the people <u>silent</u>? Shocked? Frightened?
The first rains of the monsoon were streaking vertically out of the low grey sky like a curtain, and through the cataract along the roadside	monsoon – must be in India or Far East refugees – war in India (Bangladeshi
20 came the procession of refugees.	independence?) or Vietnam? Cambodia?

James Cameron: *An Indian Summer*

Speculating

Make similar notes as you read this poem. It is telling a story, but in a way that requires you to become a detective. There are some prompt questions beside the poem to get you started, but you should be able to ask many more questions of your own. By the time you have finished, you should be able to work out the main points of the story behind the clues the poet gives.

The drawer

Their belongings were buried side by side
In a shallow bureau drawer. There was her
Crocodile handbag, letters, a brooch,
All that was in the bedside cupboard
5   And a small green jar she'd had for flowers.

My father's were in an envelope:
A khaki lanyard, crushed handkerchief,
Twelve cigarettes, a copying-pencil,
All he had on him when he was killed
10   Or all my mother wanted to keep.

I put them together, seven years ago.
Now that we've moved, my wife and I,
To a house of our own, I've taken them out.
Until we can find another spare drawer
15   They're packed in a cardboard box in the hall.

So this dead, middle-aged, middle-class man
Killed by a misfired shell, and his wife
Dead of cirrhosis, have left one son
Aged nine, aged nineteen, aged twenty-six,
20   Who has buried them both in a cardboard box.

George MacBeth

- Who are *they*?

- What is a lanyard?
- So what had the father been doing when he was killed?

- What happened seven years ago?

- What is cirrhosis and what causes it?

- How do you *bury* people *in a cardboard box* – what does he mean?

Paraphrasing

The extract on the Mississippi is short and apparently quite straightforward. Make sure that you have understood it fully by writing a paraphrase, expressing its meaning fully in your own words.

Mississippi riverboat pilot

A pilot must have a memory; but there are two higher qualities which he must also have. He must have good and quick judgement and decision, and a cool, calm courage that no peril can shake. Give a man the merest trifle of pluck to start with, and by the time
5   he has become a pilot he cannot be unmanned by any danger a steamboat can get into; but one cannot quite say the same for judgement. Judgement is a matter of brains, and a man must *start* with a good stock of that article or he will never succeed as a pilot.

Mark Twain: *Life on the Mississippi*

A13 Building a story

What is the story?

The pictures on this page and the next tell the first part of a story, but they have been printed in the wrong order. Can you arrange them so that they tell a story that makes sense?

5

6

7

8

9

1 Plot

The plot is the list of events in the order in which they happened, including any links between them – if one event causes another, for example.

2 Character

Most stories involve one or more characters. As the story evolves, the reader usually gets to know these people better, through:

- their words
- their actions
- what other characters say about them
- what the storyteller says about them.

See unit A20, page 62.

3 Setting

Where and when the story takes place are often very important. This has to be communicated to the reader:

- directly, through description
- indirectly by the way in which the characters speak about the place and time, and the way in which they behave.

As with character, the setting of the story will not work unless it has been fully imagined by the writer.

4 Viewpoint

When you tell a story you can choose the 'voice' with which you tell it to the reader. For example you may 'speak' as yourself, as one of the characters, or as some other invented person who knows about the story. The viewpoint you choose affects the tone of voice you adopt when you tell the story.

See unit A22, page 70.

5 Story

The story is the way in which the events are revealed to the reader by the storyteller. This may be the same as the order in which they happened, or it may be different.

See unit A21, page 66.

6 Format

Stories can be told in many different ways. For example:

- as a straightforward narrative
- using different storytellers to tell their own version of events
- using only or mainly conversation
- using letters and other documents to tell part or all of the story.

What to do

1 Use the pictures on pages 39 and 40 as the basis for a story. Write a plot outline of the whole story.

2 Make detailed notes on each of the characters in your story.

3 Make detailed notes on the settings for your story.

4 Decide who is going to tell your story.

5 Decide on the order in which the story will be told.

6 Decide on the format you are going to use.

7 **Now tell your story.**

A14 Almost as if you were there ...

Writing description

Writing good descriptive prose is not easy. You need to:

1. observe accurately, using as many of your senses as you can
2. remember the details you have observed
3. know clearly who you are writing for
4. have a distinct idea of what you are trying to achieve in your description – why you want your reader to read it
5. use your intelligence and imagination to bring all the separate elements of your topic together
6. find the words to help the reader 'see' what you are describing.

Observing

Look carefully at the photographs on these two pages. Try to gain as strong an impression as you can of the place they depict.

When you are ready, turn to the next page, **but be warned: you will be asked to write without looking again at the pictures!**

La Rochelle

The photographs you have been looking at show The Old Port at La Rochelle in western France.

1 Without looking back at the photographs, write down the things that most struck you about the place. Make your notes as full and as detailed as you can.

2 Look at the photographs again carefully. Make a list of all the details you notice, which might be useful when writing a description.

3 Imagine that you are standing on the quayside. Write a list of what you can:

- see
- hear
- feel
- smell.

4 Now choose one of the writing topics and use your ideas as the basis for a piece of descriptive writing about La Rochelle.

Writing topics

- At the beginning of a short story, the central character is lost in this area, separated from the person(s) they were with. Describe the character's impressions, thoughts, and feelings and what they see as they wander round.
- A trip has been arranged by a local primary school for Primary 6 pupils starting French. They are to be given a detailed itinerary and description, with no illustrations, of all the places they are going visit. Write a description of The Old Harbour at La Rochelle to give them an idea of what kind of place it is and what they can expect to see.

Comparing notes

On the opposite page are three descriptions of different towns by widely different writers.

- Read all three carefully and try to visualise the places they describe.
- Read them again and look at the ways in which each writer tries to communicate the atmosphere of the place they are describing.
- Write brief answers to each of these questions:

  1 What are the good points of each text?
  2 What are the bad points (if any) of each?
  3 If you had to place them in order, with the best first, what order would you put them in and why?

- Now write a paragraph about the text you have chosen as the best, explaining the reasons for your choice.

Ávila

Ávila is the highest city in Spain – it is also one of the country's most enchanting, a medieval walled town of great presence. If you arrive at dusk, the walls are softly illuminated. Built of dark granite in the last decade of the 11th century, they stretch for some two-and-a-half kilometres, crenellated and enclosing Ávila in a powerful stone rectangle, 12 metres high and three metres thick.

Every 25 metres or so Ávila's walls are buttressed by towers, 88 in all. Nine monumental gates, defended by sturdy turrets, pierce these walls. Two, the Puerta de Alcázar and the Puerta de San Vicente, are outstanding. Others, such as the venerable and ineffectual Madrigal de las Altas Torres, seem to have forgotten why they were first built.

James Bentley: *Hello*

Airdrie, 1935

It was a warm, overcast summer day; groups of idle, sullen-looking young men stood at the street corners; smaller groups were wandering among the blue-black ranges of pit-dumps which in that region are the substitute for nature; the houses looked empty and unemployed like their tenants; and the road along which the car stumbled was pitted and rent, as if it had recently been under shell-fire. Everything had the look of a Sunday which had lasted for many years, during which the bells had forgotten to ring and the Salvation Army, with its accordions and concertinas, had gone into seclusion, so that one did not even trouble to put on one's best clothes: a disused, slovenly everlasting Sunday. The open shops had an unconvincing and yet illicit look, and the few black-dusted miners whom I saw trudging home seemed hardly to believe in their own existence. The scene actually evoked a sense of peace: the groups quietly talking at the street corners or walking among the pit-dumps, the shafts rising smokeless, and the neglected roads.

Edwin Muir: *Scottish Journey*

Guatemala City in the 1970s

It was a brutal city, but at six in the morning a froth of fog endowed it with a secrecy and gave it the simplicity of a mountain-top. Before the sun rose to burn it away, the fog dissolved the dull straight lines of its streets, and whitened its low houses and made its sombre people ghostly as they appeared for moments before being lifted away, like revengers glimpsed in their hauntings. Then Guatemala City, such a grim thing, became a tracing, a sketch without substance, and the poor Indians and peasants – who had no power – looked blue and bold and watchful. They possessed it at this hour. There was no wind; the fog hung in fine grey clouds, a foot from the ground. Even the railway station, no more than a brick shed, took on the character of a great terminus: there was no way of verifying that it did not rise up for five storeys in a clock tower crowned by pigeons and iron-work, so well-hidden was its small tin roof by the fog the volcanoes had trapped.

Paul Theroux: *The Old Patagonian Express*

A15 The shipwright

Explaining

A story tells you what happened and a description tells you what something or someone is like. An explanation tells you:

- how to do something
- how something works, or what something or someone does.

A good explanation:

- is aware of the problems the audience may have in following what is being explained
- makes sure that any words or ideas that are likely to be difficult are introduced carefully and explained thoroughly
- divides the topic up into clear sections and presents them in the best possible order
- does not go through things so quickly that the audience cannot keep up.

The text that follows is part of the transcript of an interview with Adrian Wombwell, a shipwright. Read the text and look at the pictures, then follow the instructions at the end.

A A shipwright is a person that can work on any sort of boat. I specialise in a construction called clinker, where the planks are overlapped, as opposed to carvel, where the planks are butted up to each other. It's a specific type of boat that's used in this area – in East Anglia.   5

B We live by the coast in Essex, on an estuary, the River Blackwater, and there's quite a big marina there and I do all my work in the marina. There's also a company that installs Volvo engines and I do all the work for them, making engine covers, instrument panels –   10 anything that they might need when they fit a new engine into a boat …

C I have a boat-building shed, a workshop, which has been used for generations as a workshop for boatbuilding … it's 48 feet by 18, and it's a wooden   15 weatherboard building with quite large doors on each end to enable me to get quite big boats in. I've got a planer-thicknesser, a bandsaw and a circular saw and all the hand tools that I need: routers, electric planers, sanders, disk-cutters – plus all the handtools,   20 traditional handtools: adzes, drawknives, planes. It's quite a specialised job and there's a lot of specialised tools that are just used for boatbuilding … it takes a long time to be able to use them properly.

D There's all manner of repairs. People are forever coming and saying, 'Can you fix this? 25
I've broken this. I've broken my mast … I've broken my rudder'. And then interiors of
boats. I've fitted out old working boats. I did one recently, a smack, and it had never
ever had an interior in it and I put an entire interior in the boat …

E I have people that have problems – they might
be sailing down the coast. There was an
instance quite recently where a boat started 30
leaking badly, so they came into Tollesbury. They
phoned the marina and said, 'Is there anybody
that can help us?' And I said, 'Yes,' so they
brought the boat in. The boat was hauled out 35
and I repaired the problem. It was leaking along
the garboard plank, the plank at the bottom. We
re-caulked it and the man went back in the
water the next day and sailed off …

F People like to change the interior of their boat – they might buy a new boat and there are things that they're not happy with; they want things altered. So I've made tables for boats, chart tables, and altered the interior – you might move the bunks from one side to the other, make things bigger and smaller … 40

G I used to sell trucks and vans which was a pretty tedious job, really. It involved charging round the countryside. With this job I can please myself. It's a satisfying thing to do, to be able to work with wood which is a really nice medium – and there's not so much pressure. I don't have to travel either; I just walk a few hundred yards from my house … and you meet some really interesting people. 45

Getting a grasp of the material

1 The text has been divided into seven lettered sections. Write down the letter of each and next to it a few words summing up what that section contains.

2 Which section(s) tell(s) the reader about each of the following?

  a where he works
  b the types of work he does
  c the equipment he uses
  d the repairs he does
  e his thoughts and feelings about his work.

3 Make a list of the technical terms he uses and against each one write a short definition. If possible work these out from the context; if not, use a dictionary.

4 Look carefully at the photographs. Write any additional information they give about Adrian and his work.

Preparing to write

You have been asked to write 150–200 words for a directory of local craftspeople explaining what Adrian Wombwell does.

5 Make a list of 3–5 key points you need to cover. These will form the basis of 3–5 paragraphs in your writing.

6 For each key point make a list of the main information you need to include.

7 Decide on the order in which you want to present your material.

Writing

8 Write a first draft of your explanation. Do this without referring to the printed text or photographs.

9 Check your draft against the text and photographs:

  ■ make sure that you have not missed out anything important
  ■ check your writing against the definition of a 'good explanation' on page 46.

10 Rewrite your explanation, changing it as necessary.

A16 *What do you think?*

Argument and persuasion

When you put across a point of view, you may feel strongly about the subject. It is good to be able to argue with conviction. Two other things are also important:

- you must be able to express clearly the point of view you want to put across and that means knowing clearly what you believe
- you must be able to back up each main point you make with:
  – a supporting argument, or
  – factual evidence.

Outlaw this killer sport

New calls for ban after knocked-out boxer dies

These two headlines appeared in national newspapers shortly after a boxing match in which a boxer, James Murray, died after being knocked out. While he was being cared for by doctors in the ring, fighting broke out amongst the spectators, some of whom were drunk. The events led to a debate in the press and on radio and television about whether boxing should be banned. On pages 50 and 51 the opposing arguments are presented.

1 Read both arguments through.
2 Read them a second time, this time making a careful note of the main points and the evidence or reasoning. Choose your own way of doing this, or use a chart like this:

AGAINST	
Point	Evidence or Reasoning
More dangerous than other sports	It is the only sport in which the main aim is to inflict physical damage on

Which of them puts forward a better argument?
Has either of them persuaded you to change your mind?

'Noble art' is man's right

By **JULIAN CRITCHLEY** Conservative MP for Aldershot

THE DEATH of James Murray, following so closely upon that of the boxer Bradley Stone, and the terrible neurological injuries suffered by Michael Watson and Gerald
5 McClennan, cannot fail to strengthen the belief of all those who would ban boxing.

Those of us who enjoy the 'noble art' have been placed on the defensive. How can we justify a 'sport', the purpose of
10 which is to inflict injury upon an opponent?

I should first acknowledge that reforms should be made. Championship fights have already been reduced from 15 to 12
15 rounds (Murray collapsed in the 12th).

Why not reduce them still further to 10, leaving the run-of-the-mill fight to eight rounds? The gloves could be made heavier and, most important perhaps of all, alcohol
20 should be banned from the boxing arena.

The death of Murray was made more likely by the riot, with drunken fans throwing bottles into the ring, thus preventing the first-aid teams from reaching the strick-
25 en fighter in good time.

Were boxing to be banned by Act of Parliament, the sport would be driven underground where it would thrive without supervision, medical or otherwise.

The British Boxing Board of Control, of 30 which I was a member for several years, has done much to improve the medical attention a fighter receives both before and after a fight, and precautions have been taken to alleviate the consequences of neu- 35 rological injury.

Hospitals are alerted before a fight, and trained paramedics are made available when the bout takes place.

In a free society a young man should 40 have the right to fight if he wants to make boxing his career.

Injuries are no more common than they are in motor racing and football; more people die of exposure each year climbing 45 in the Scottish and Welsh highlands than they do boxing for a living.

Boxing is banned in Norway and Sweden but their fighters perform in Denmark, the United States and even 50 Britain.

Boxing is, for many tough kids, the quickest way out of the ghetto.

Henry Cooper is a national hero. Should he have been prevented from doing 55 what he could do best? Of course not.

Murray's death is a tragedy, but boxing should not be banned as a consequence of it.

The Daily Express

Time to ring the last bell

By **DR VIVIENNE NATHANSON** Head of policy at the BMA

ONCE again a boxer has died after a knockout punch in the ring. Another family bereaved, more blanket media coverage, including more calls for improve-
5 ments in medical attention at the ringside and for better safety measures.

All this is missing the point. Any new safety measures are simply tinkering at the edges – boxing cannot be made safe
10 unless the head is taken out of the target area.

Up until now the consensus with the sport's defenders and promoters has always been that people have a choice
15 whether to box or not, that they are not forced into the ring, that boxers know the risks involved.

Yet what choice is there really? Are we so brutal a society that we encourage a
20 sport which offers the combatants a choice between long-term brain damage following many fights and immediate brain damage or death following a knockout punch?
25 Those with long boxing careers who have not suffered in this way are just lucky, in the same way that 80-year-olds in good health after smoking 40 a day are not an advertisement for the benefits of
30 tobacco.

There are injuries in other sports and doctors are always looking for better pro-
tection from sports injuries, but boxing stands alone as the only sport where the prime objective is to inflict maximum 35 damage on the opponent.

The involvement of television and the glamorising of the proceedings have led to an increased emphasis on the knockout punch. 40

In view of the overwhelming evidence against boxing, the BMA has been calling for a ban on professional boxing since 1982, with further policies to ban amateur and schoolboy boxing following over the 45 years.

We are not out on a limb, as most other medical associations in the world have the same policies, and in countries where the sport is already banned it has not gone 50 underground as is always predicted by the boxing fraternity.

It may be that the tide against boxing is finally turning. Sports writers no longer ridicule the BMA's position and this week- 55 end even Frank Warren the boxing promoter has said he felt he could no longer defend the sport to James Murray's family.

It is up to society as a whole to decide whether it wants to ring the final bell on 60 boxing, or simply to take a ringside seat as more young men die or suffer permanent brain damage in the name of sport.

The Daily Express

BMA: British Medical Association

Congested Britain: the driver's choice?

The problem: we all want to have our own car and drive it whenever we please, but we all want to live in uncongested and unpolluted streets.

What do you think is the solution?

1 Make a chart like this. Fill in as many ideas and arguments as you can.
2 Decide where **you** stand on this problem.
3 Use the material you have collected to write a convincing argument expressing your point of view.

Plan and draft your argument carefully: there is more about this in unit A7 on pages 24–25.

Possible solution	For	Against
Make 'Park & Ride' schemes compulsory and ban private cars in town centres	big reduction in pollution + congestion	not enough space for car parks very unpopular
Improve roads and build more by-passes		
Improve public transport		
Make road taxes much higher		
Raise the price of petrol		

A17 The challenge

Writing letters

Modern technology now offers us many different ways to send messages to other people. Even so, the 'old-fashioned' letter still has a number of important advantages:

- it is cheap
- it is easy to use
- it provides a permanent record of the message.

People still use letters for many different purposes. These may be:

- **official:** for example, an application for a job
- **personal:** for example, a letter to a friend you have not seen for some time
- **informal:** for example, a note left for a person you called on but who is out.

Each of these has its own:

- layout
- approach
- style.

This unit is based on an imaginary letter-writing competition. Read the material on pages 53–55 and then follow the instructions on page 55.

the
Logi-sticks Challenge

Are you a winner?
Going to college? **16+?**
Staying on in the 6th form? **Short of cash?**

If so, Logi-sticks want to hear from you. We have money to give away to six promising students – money for books, equipment, clothing, to help you through the next two years. Send for the information pack and then just write us a letter explaining why **you** are the person we are looking for. The best six letters will win.

Logi-sticks
Unit 4
Lanark Estate
Flemington

Logi-sticks

16+ letter competition briefing

The company

We wholesale and distribute industrial adhesives – everything from twinpack polymer resins to transparent adhesive tape. We have a fully-mechanised, fully-computerised warehouse, covering 2,500m^2. We distribute throughout Great Britain using our own fleet of articulated lorries.

What we are offering

We will provide financial support to provide textbooks, personal study materials, a personal computer and software, clothing and other equipment necessary for school or college.

What we are looking for

A student who is lively, intelligent and looking to the future. A person who has good interpersonal skills and is not easily 'thrown'. In return for the support we offer, you would undertake to do two 4-week paid placements (work experience) during your summer holidays.

What to do

Write us a letter about yourself. Tell us about:
- your educational background
- your interests
- your hopes and plans for the future
- why you are the person we are looking for.

The details

Your letter should be handwritten. It should be addressed to Michael Grayling, Director of Human Resources, Logi-sticks. The text of the letter should be between 200 and 300 words in length.

Dear Sir or Madam,

In response to your recent interesting and generous offer in last week's copy of the Flemington Advertiser, I should like to offer my services to Logi-sticks. I have
5   known about your company for some time and consider it to be a notable market leader.

     Although I am still at school and studying for my Standard Grade examinations, I am planning a successful career in business. I am taking 8 Standard
10   Grades, including Maths, Physics and Chemistry, and I expect to acquire good grades in all of them.

Dear Michael,

Yes please! I want to put my name forward for this fantastic offer by Logi-sticks.

     Let me introduce myself. My name is Edward
5   Massey and I'm in fourth year at Flemington High. I am doing Standard Grades this term and am taking six subjects. I reckon I stand a good chance of getting top grades in all of them. Well, I can dream, can't I?
10   But seriously, Michael, about this offer of yours. I think I'm just the person you're looking for. In addition to a good brain, I . . .

Dear Mr Grayling,

I should like to put my name forward for the Logi-sticks Challenge.
I am a student at St Michael's High School, Flemington, and am about to
take my Standard Grades. I am entered for seven subjects, including
English, Maths, Chemistry and Physics. My teachers say I have a good
chance of gaining band 1 passes in at least four subjects, including
English and Maths. I am planning to stay on at school to study English
and Communication, Maths and Economics at Higher level. I have chosen
these subjects because I think they will give me a good balanced
background in preparation for some form of higher education.

A winner?

Is any of these three letters likely to be a winner? Make a detailed comparison of the three extracts and place them in order of merit. Pay particular attention to:

- **content:** what each one says
- **structure:** the order in which it says it. You only have the beginning of each letter; what do you think about each of these as the introduction to quite a long letter?
- **tone:** the way in which the writers address their audience.

You try

Write your own letter of application, using the following advice.

Content

1 Read the advertisement and briefing again carefully.
2 Make a list of the different types of information that are requested.
3 For each type make a list of the main points you need to make.

Structure

It is very important to get the **order** of a letter right. Every letter must have:

- a **beginning**, in which you make clear what the letter is about. Look again at the sample letters and see how each writer did this.
- a **middle**, in which you set out the main points you wish to make.
- an **ending**, in which you 'say goodbye' to the reader(s), but aim to leave them with a clear idea of what you would like them to do – and also with positive feelings towards you.

Each of these sections should have at least one paragraph devoted to it. The middle will often take a number of paragraphs.

Tone

This isn't just a matter of the correct greeting and ending; it is a matter of how the letter 'sounds'. When you have written the first draft of your letter, try reading it aloud. As you do so, imagine the person you are addressing, sitting reading it. Will they finish it with positive feelings towards you?

A18 Writing a newspaper report

Researching the story

There are seven questions that journalists ask when they are researching a story.

WHO (or what) is the story about?
WHAT occurred?
WHERE did it take place?
WHEN did it take place?
HOW did it happen?
WHY did it happen?
WHAT do people say/think about it?

Organising the story

A newspaper story is written in a different way from most stories. Normally you start at the beginning and go on until you get to the end. Journalists tell the whole story briefly in the first paragraph or two. Then they add in the details in the rest of the article. This is not as silly as it sounds. Often people only want the main details. If you get that at the start, you can decide whether or not you want to read more. Hardly anyone wants to read a paper from cover to cover, so this way of writing helps people to choose.

Main story
Detail
Background

Writing the story

The way in which people read newspapers affects the **style** of writing too. Stories are usually written:

- in short paragraphs
- in simple, direct sentences.

To give a report more punch, journalists often:

- miss out words like 'a', 'an', 'the'
- use noun phrases which help to string a lot of ideas together in a short space:

   '**Prime Minister Tony Blair** said today …'

Anatomy of a newspaper report

Master offers chance to be an Ettrick shepherd for the weekend

William Chisholm

For centuries, the secrets of shepherding have been passed down through generations.

Now, one of Scotland's leading exponents of the skill is developing a centre of excellence in the Borders.

Bobby Dalziel, a double winner of the International, the top event on the British trialling calendar, and three times Scottish champion, believes the popularity of *One Man and His Dog* will ensure the success of the Ettrick Sheep Dog and Hill Walking Centre.

The centre, at Potburn, close to the top end of the valley where James Hogg, the original Ettrick Shepherd, tended sheep and wrote his prose and poetry 200 years ago, is not due to open until next May. But Mr Dalziel already has a list of clients who want to be shepherds for a weekend.

His centre will stand close to the Southern Upland Way, the walking route linking Scotland's west and east coasts.

The area is full of wildlife and the facilities will offer an ideal base for birdwatchers and hill walkers. The working sheep farm will also offer access to 2,500 acres of hill country. Mr Dalziel will also be passing on his skill and experience to young shepherds and their dogs who will enrol for residential courses.

He said: 'We will be able to cater for people whether they have their own sheepdog or not. There is a young dog here which the tourists can work with. I issue most of my orders by whistling with the help of my fingers, but we will even have plastic whistles which are just as effective.'

The recent lifting of quarantine restrictions in Europe now allows shepherds and dogs from overseas to use the Scottish centre. Special competitions will be organised.

Mr Dalziel, originally from Ayrshire, picked up the basics of shepherding from older men in the locality.

He started running dogs in 1975 and won the Scottish shepherds' championship four years later. The Scottish title was his in 1986 and again in 1992 and 1995. The victories in the International in 1989 and 1992 were undoubtedly his finest achievements in an outstanding career.

He said: 'Although I have been at Potburn for 16 years I only started farming for myself in February this year. We will continue to run about 8,000 head of sheep on the farm so there will be opportunities for visitors to see how a unit like this works.

'Many who come here will do so for fun. But there will be an educational aspect, with parties from schools and colleges welcome at our centre.'

• *Bobby Dalziel will share his skills with the common herd*

The Scotsman

---

1 **Headline**
Usually added by a sub-editor who also checks a reporter's work and cuts it to the right length.

2 **Lead**
The first paragraph or two (often in bold or large type) which gives the main facts, especially **WHO**, **WHAT**, **WHEN**.

3 **Photograph**
Helps to bring story alive.

4 **Byline**
The name(s) of the reporter(s) who wrote the story.

5 **Caption**
Explaining the photograph.

Problem child

You are a reporter on a local paper and this is a page from your notebook. You have been given the information over the phone by a colleague. Now you are going to follow up the story. Read the notes and then follow the instructions.

- allegations that an eight-year-old boy attacks other children:
  - attacks pensioners
  - throws stones at windows
  - rips up plants/bushes/trees
- allegations that nine-year-old sister is also involved
- complaints from fourteen neighbours in Ayr
- have contacted police
- response: 'We are taking the complaints seriously'
- age of the children means that the police cannot take action
- there has been a referral to the Reporter to the Children's Panel
- the Children's Panel met yesterday : possibility of taking into care
- matter has been brought to the attention of local MSP John Scott
- children cannot be named for legal reasons

A Researching the story

1 Which of the seven questions on page 56 have been answered:

   a in a satisfactory way?
   b partly, but not fully?
   c not at all?

2 Think about the details that you have obtained and make up the answers to the questions that still need answering.

B Organising the story

3 Make a brief plan for your report, following the pattern described on page 56. Number the paragraphs and list briefly the information that each will contain.

4 Check your plan by writing the first paragraph.

C Writing the story

5 Now write a first draft of the story, following the advice on style given on page 56.

6 When you have written it, think of a suitable headline. Remember that newspaper headlines are designed to catch the reader's eye and often make use of:

   - alliteration – having two or more words starting with the same letter (for example 'Bully Boy')
   - puns – playing on words.

Work with a partner.

7 Exchange drafts with your partner. Read and comment on each other's work.

8 Write a final draft taking note of the comments that your partner made.

A19 Writing an article

> An article is a piece of deliberately structured writing for publication ... which aims to inform, comment, persuade or entertain. It might aim to inspire or to stimulate the reader to think, or to provoke to action. An article often includes the author's point of view, and sometimes develops an argument.
>
> **Brendan Hennessy**: Writing feature articles

In school you may be asked by a teacher or examiner to write an article, or you might write one for a school magazine. In each case there are certain things you always have to think about.

purpose
(look at the box at the top of this page)

ARTICLE

subject
Do you need to do research before writing?

audience
(see unit A9 on page 29)

Structure and style

More often than not, people read articles for pleasure and they can easily lose interest and turn over the page to something more entertaining. So the writer must work hard to capture and retain the readers' interest. Key features of how this is done are shown on page 60.

Looking at the example

1 How does the writer attempt to catch – and keep – our interest in the first paragraph?
2 How does the second paragraph link with the first?
3 There are nine paragraphs. Read the whole article again and make sure that you have a clear idea of the subject matter of each. Then draw up a table like this, and fill each column.

Number	What it is about	Key sentence/part of sentence	Possible title
1	How paintball was invented	Paintball ... and North America	How it all began

WAR GAMES

Every weekend thousands of men (and a few women) don camouflage gear and head for the woods clutching high-powered weapons. Paintballing is big business – but what kind of person gets a kick from playing at killing?

As you grind your face into the dirt and try to summon up that elusive killer instinct, with missiles whizzing over your head, remember this: you owe it all to the back end of a cow. Paintball, now a multi-million pound business, was born in the early 1980s in Canada and North America, when ranchers who branded their cattle by shooting pellets of indelible paint at them, discovered as all good cowboys do, that it was rather more fun shooting each other.

The oil-based paint was exchanged for water-based vegetable dye, a few basic rules were established and the game – then called Survival – was on. In 1984 it was franchised to England and was soon joined by a second version called Skirmish. A third company, Mayhem Paintball, was set up in 1985 – it's now the biggest.

Today paintball is Britain's fastest-growing sport with more than 40,000 dedicated gunslingers. The word has spread far and wide, and teams are now blasting each other black, blue and dayglo pink in South Africa, Australia, the Far East – and even, surprisingly, in Beirut.

During the economic boom years of the late 1980s paintball became a favourite recreation of many large companies. Imagine 80 or 100 estate agents paintballing at a time. (Get out the real guns, you're probably saying.)

Corporate days out are about more than the chance to splat the boss with paint. The idea is to 'create a new dynamic among the staff' – a way of working together that might not be apparent in the structured work environment. A day rushing about taking pot-shots at others prevents more serious memo-borne salvoes across the desks. 'It's a great leveller,' says Paul Wilson, a director of Mayhem. We can vouch for that.

Unfortunately for paintball organisers, the recession put paid to many of these excursions.

Semi-professional paintball, however, flourishes. There are currently three leagues in Britain – Northern, Midland and Home Counties – each made up of about 40 teams of ten players. Although paintball is played all year round, there is, as in football and cricket, a tournament season, which runs from autumn until May. The climax of the season is the Mayhem Open, when 60 teams from all over the world descend on Hellingly in Sussex to compete for a prize of £70,000. (This year, much to the chagrin of the British, the Americans won.)

Look at any paintball magazine – there are two currently on sale in this country – and you could be forgiven for thinking most players have either just walked off the set of *Apocalypse Now* or failed to get into the SAS on psychiatric grounds. The teams have names like Delta Force and Punishers, and play with guns that look far more like the real thing than the real thing does. 'Most players are ordinary working people like you and I,' reassures Paul Wilson. 'The non-macho types far outweigh the macho'.

'The 'Nam types don't last long,' adds Rob Honnington, also of Mayhem. 'You can't have a bunch of blokes just running around shooting at anything. There are rules'. Indeed there are, to ensure safety and fair play, although they vary from country to country and interpretation in the heat of battle causes many an argument.

You don't have to be supremely fit or even able-bodied to play paintball. Disabled people are just as capable of firing a pump-action shotgun as anyone else, and many centres have appropriate facilities. The game is open to children too (though, for insurance reasons, they must be over 12). Youngsters usually play in their own groups. But they can mix it with the adults – and, as the *Focus* team discovered, be every bit as dastardly.
CAROLINE ELLIOTT

Introduction
Leads in to the subject in an interesting and thought-provoking way.

Paragraphs
The article is divided into paragraphs. Each one develops one aspect of the subject clearly. Paragraphs are kept quite short.

Linking
The writer makes links between paragraphs, so that the reader is led smoothly through the article.

Conclusion
Rounds off the article in an interesting way so that the reader goes away satisfied. (And, in this case, since the article is the beginning of a magazine section devoted to the subject, it leads naturally in to the rest of the section.)

Making connections

In a good piece of writing there are neat links between paragraphs. One paragraph ends with a sentence that allows the next one to be linked to it without making a big fuss about it. One of these links is marked on page 60: the question of the need to be 'macho' in paragraph 7 is linked to the idea at the beginning of paragraph 8 of ''Nam types' (people who fantasise that they are fighting in the Vietnam war).

Other examples
Look again at the article and see how each paragraph is linked to the next.

Write an article

1 Choose a subject:

 ■ take one from the list of topics, or
 ■ think of a topic of your own.

2 Decide where your article is to be published. Write notes describing your audience, subject matter and purpose.
3 Make a detailed plan of the structure of your article. (See unit A7 on page 24 for further guidance on this.)
4 Write the article.

Topics

Experiences
Think of something that has happened to you that is unusual, frightening, exciting, amusing.

Strongly-held beliefs
What really makes you angry or upset? Write about it in a way that persuades other people to your point of view.

Phobias
Most people are frightened of something. Either write about your own fears, or do some research and write about other people's. (Look at the list below.)

Phobias

acrophobia	fear of heights	nosophobia	fear of disease
aerophobia	fear of air travel	odontophobia	fear of going to the dentist
agoraphobia	fear of open or public spaces	ombrophobia	fear of rain
arachnophobia	fear of spiders	ornithophobia	fear of birds
autophobia	fear of being alone	osphresiophobia	fear of body odour
claustrophobia	fear of enclosed spaces	pantophobia	fear of everything
erotophobia	fear of sex	pediophobia	fear of dolls
gynophobia	fear of women	phobophobia	fear of being afraid
homilophobia	fear of sermons	social phobia	fear of being watched in public
microphobia	fear of small objects	trypanophobia	fear of injections

A20 What was he like?

Character

We can learn about characters in stories from:

- what the storyteller tells us about them and their thoughts
- what they say
- what they do
- what other characters say or think about them
  (although they may not always tell the truth).

Writing a character study

When we write about characters, we can describe:

- what they look like
- how they behave
- what their personalities are like
- the way in which they change during the story.

In each case we must back up what we say by referring to
one of the points in the Character list above.

This unit focuses on the strong central
character in a short story. As you work
through it, make notes of your responses,
because at the end you will be asked to
write a detailed character study.

First sight

Of all the teachers in the school Waldo was
the one who commanded the most respect. In
his presence nobody talked, with the result that
he walked the corridors in a moat of silence.
5 Boys seeing him approach would drop their
voices to a whisper and only when he was out
of earshot would they speak normally again.

First impression

What strikes you most about
this introduction to the
character of Waldo?

Reading

Between classes there was always five minutes' uproar. The boys wrestled over
desks, shouted, whistled, flung books while some tried to learn their nouns, eyes
10 closed, feet tapping to the rhythm of declensions. Others put frantic finishing
touches to the last night's exercise. Some minutes before Waldo's punctual arrival,
the class quietened. Three rows of boys, all by now strumming nouns, sat hunched
and waiting.

Waldo's entrance was theatrical. He strode in with strides as long as his soutane
15 would permit, his books clenched in his left hand and pressed tightly against his
chest. With his right hand he swung the door behind him, closing it with a crash.
His eyes raked the class. If, as occasionally happened, it did not close properly he
did not turn from the class but backed slowly against the door snapping it shut
with his behind. Two strides brought him to the rostrum. He cracked his books
20 down with an explosion and made a swift palm upward gesture.

Waldo was very tall, his height being emphasised by the soutane, narrow and
tight-fitting at the shoulders, sweeping down like a bell to the floor. A row of
black, gleaming buttons bisected him from floor to throat. When he talked his
Adam's apple hit against the hard, white Roman collar and created in Kevin the
25 same sensation as a fingernail scraping down the blackboard. His face was sallow
and immobile. (There was a rumour that he had a glass eye but no-one knew
which. Nobody could look at him long enough because to meet his stare was to
invite a question.) He abhorred slovenliness. Once when presented with an untidy
exercise book, dog-eared with a tea-ring on the cover, he picked it up, the corner
30 of one leaf between his finger and thumb, the pages splaying out like a fan,
opened the window and dropped it three floors to the ground. His own neatness
became exaggerated when he was at the board, writing in copperplate script just
large enough for the boy in the back row to read – geometrical columns of
declined nouns defined by exact, invisible margins. When he had finished, he
35 would set the chalk down and rub the used finger and thumb together with the
same action he used after handling the host over the paten.

Response

What have you learned about these aspects of the character of Father Waldo?

- his appearance – his face
  – his clothing
- his behaviour – how he moved about the room
  – how he used his hands
- what he was like as a person.

Make sure that you can support each point you make with a reference to the text.

The story from which these extracts are taken concerns a young boy, Kevin Sweeny, and his Latin teacher, the priest Father Waldo. Kevin has been helped with his Latin homework by his father. Unfortunately, not only has he got all the answers wrong, but he has blurted out that he was sure they were right because his father said so. The teacher mockingly echoes Kevin's words.

Reading

'Because my father said so.' This time the commotion in the class was obvious.

'And where does your father teach Latin?' There was no escape. Waldo had
40   him. He knew now there would be an exhibition for the class. Kevin placed his weight on his arm and felt his tremble communicated to the desk.

'He doesn't, Father.'

'And what does he do?'

Kevin hesitated, stammering,
45   'He's a barman.'

'A barman!' Waldo mimicked and the class roared loudly.

'*Quiet.*' He wheeled on them. 'You, Sweeny. Come out here.' He reached inside the breast of his soutane and with a flourish produced a thin yellow cane, whipping it back and forth, testing it.
50   Kevin walked out to the front of the class, his face fiery red, the blood throbbing in his ears. He held out his hand. Waldo raised it higher, more to his liking, with the tip of the cane touching the underside of the upturned palm. He held it there for some time.

'If your brilliant father continues to do your homework for you, Sweeny,
55   you'll end up a barman yourself.' Then he whipped the cane down expertly across the tips of his fingers and again just as the blood began to surge back into them. Each time the cane in its follow-through cracked loudly against the skirts of his soutane.

'You could have made a better job of it yourself. Other hand.' The same
60   ritual of raising and lowering the left hand with the tip of the cane to the desired height. 'After all, I have taught you some Latin.' *Crack.* 'It would be hard to do any worse.'

Response

■ What additional information and ideas do we learn about Waldo from this section of the story?

■ Does it make any major changes to our impressions of the teacher, or just add to them?

Reading

As the bell rang Waldo gathered up his books and said, 'Sweeny, I want a word with you outside. '*Ave Maria, gratia plena …*' It was not until the end of
65   the corridor that Waldo turned to face him. He looked at Kevin and maintained his silence for a moment.

'Sweeny, I must apologise to you.' Kevin bowed his head. 'I meant your father no harm – he's probably a good man, a very good man.'

'Yes, sir,' said Kevin. The pain in his fingers had gone.

70 'Look at me when I'm talking, please.' Kevin looked at his collar, his Adam's apple, then his face. It relaxed for a fraction and Kevin thought he was almost going to smile, but he became efficient, abrupt again.

'All right, very good, you may go back to your class.'

'Yes Father,' Kevin nodded and moved back along the empty corridor.

Bernard MacLaverty: *Secrets*

Response

Does this short extract change your view of Waldo in any way?

Writing about character

Structure

A good character study is not just a list of qualities backed up by quotations; it is also a carefully organised piece of writing. Once you have collected your ideas and evidence, you should group them by theme. For example, you might decide to write three paragraphs about Waldo:

1 who he was – where he worked – first impressions of him as a teacher
2 the main features of his personality
3 the possibility (suggested in the last section) that there might be more to him than meets the eye.

Sentences

Because of the nature of the ideas and evidence you have collected, it is easy to write a succession of sentences like this:

Waldo is neat and rather fussy. We know this because he writes in small copperplate handwriting on the board. He is also a man of habit, because when he …

A good writer will vary the sentence structure and weave the information in without a lot of 'signposts':

His fussy copperplate handwriting on the board shows that he likes everything to be neat and tidy, as does his habit of rubbing his finger and thumb together afterwards, to remove the chalk from them.

It is a convention to use the present tense when writing character studies, although some writers prefer to use the past. The important thing is to be consistent.

Words

Another feature of a good character study is that the writer uses exactly the right word. Which of the following do you think are most appropriate for the character of Waldo?

choosy	fastidious
meticulous	carping
picky	fussy
particular	cautious
unrelenting	careful
selective	punctilious
nit-picking	discriminating
finicky	

Character study

Use the information and ideas you have gathered to write a detailed description of the character of Father Waldo.

A21 The assassin

Action

One of the key things a storyteller must do is describe action. Writers do this in different ways:

1 by directly describing what happens
2 by hinting or leaving gaps so that we have to work things out for ourselves
3 through conversation.

We need action in a story to keep it moving along, but it also has other purposes:

4 to tell us about characters (we can learn a lot from the way in which they behave)
5 to maintain tension, so that we want to go on reading
6 to develop the ideas behind the story (so, for example, if the writer wants us to believe that war is evil they will present actions that show this).

Murder didn't mean much to Raven. It was just a new job. You had to be careful. You had to use your brains. It was not a question of
5   hatred. He had only seen the Minister once: he had been pointed out to Raven as he walked down the new housing estate between the small, lit Christmas trees, an old,
10   grubby man without friends, who was said to love humanity.

This is the first paragraph of a novel. It only contains 71 words, yet it tells us a lot about the central character and gives us strong hints about what is going to happen.

- The central character, Raven, is a hired killer.
- He has been given the job of killing a politician.
- Raven seems to be a cold-blooded man who takes a 'professional' approach to his work.
- The politician is a minister with no friends and probably no real private life, who has devoted himself to his work.

The first paragraph prepares us for the action that is to follow.
The next two paragraphs continue this process.

Text

The cold wind cut Raven's face in the wide Continental street. It was a good excuse for turning the collar of his coat well above his mouth. A hare-lip was a serious handicap in his profession; it had been badly sewn in infancy, so that now the upper lip was twisted and scarred. When you carried about so easy an identification you couldn't help becoming ruthless in your methods. It had always, from the first, been necessary for Raven to eliminate a witness.

He carried an attaché case. He looked like any other youngish man going home after his work; his dark overcoat had a clerical air. He moved steadily up the street like hundreds of his kind. A tram went by, lit up in the early dusk: he didn't take it. An economical young man, you might have thought, saving money for his home. Perhaps even now he was on his way to meet his girl.

Commentary

Actions	Other information
	There is a cold wind
Raven turns up the collar of his coat	He has a hare-lip. This makes him easy to identify. It has made him a ruthless killer. He has killed before, probably several times
He is carrying a case	With his collar turned up, he looks ordinary
He walks up the street	
A tram passes him	It is evening

Now read the rest of the opening of the novel and write a similar commentary on it. The prompt questions alongside the text are designed to help you do this.

But Raven had never had a girl. The hare-lip prevented that. He had learnt, when he was very young, how repulsive it was. He turned into one of the tall grey houses and climbed the stairs, a sour bitter screwed-up figure.

■ How had he learned? What effect had it had on the development of his personality?

Outside the top flat he put down his attaché case and put on gloves. He took a pair of clippers out of his pocket and cut through the telephone wire where it ran out from above the door to the lift shaft. Then he rang the bell.

■ What does this paragraph tell us about his approach to the job?

He hoped to find the Minister alone. This little top-floor flat was the socialist's home; he lived in a poor bare solitary way and Raven had been told that his secretary always left him at half-past six; he was very considerate with his employees. But Raven was a minute too early and the Minister half an hour too late. A woman opened the door, an elderly woman with pince-nez and several gold teeth. She had her hat on and her coat was over her arm. She had been on the point of leaving and she was furious at being caught. She didn't allow him to speak, but snapped at him

■ What happens in this paragraph?
■ Why the emphasis on times?

in German, 'The Minister is engaged.'

50   He wanted to spare her, not because he minded a killing
but because his employers would prefer him not to exceed
his instructions. He held the letter of introduction out to
her silently; as long as she didn't hear his foreign voice or
see the hare-lip she was safe. She took the letter primly
55   and held it up close to her pince-nez. Good, he thought,
she's short-sighted. 'Stay where you are,' she said, and
walked back up the passage. He could hear her
disapproving governess voice, then she was back in the
passage saying, 'The Minister will see you. Follow me,
60   please.' He couldn't understand the foreign speech, but he
knew what she meant from her behaviour.

His eyes, like little concealed cameras, photographed
the room instantaneously: the desk, the easy chair, the map
on the wall, the door to the bedroom behind, the wide
65   window above the bright cold Christmas street. A small oil-
stove was all the heating, and the Minister was having it
used now to boil a saucepan. A kitchen alarm-clock on the
desk marked seven o'clock. A voice said, 'Emma, put in
another egg.' The Minister came out from the bedroom.
70   He had tried to tidy himself, but he had forgotten the
cigarette ash on his trousers, and his fingers were ink-
stained. The secretary took an egg out of one of the
drawers in the desk. 'And the salt. Don't forget the salt,'
the Minister said. He explained in slow English, 'It
75   prevents the shell cracking. Sit down, my friend. Make
yourself at home. Emma, you can go.'

Raven sat down and fixed his eyes on the Minister's
chest. He thought: I'll give her three minutes by the alarm-
clock to get well away: he kept his eyes on the Minister's
80   chest: just there I'll shoot. He let his coat collar fall and
saw with bitter rage how the old man turned away from the
sight of his hare-lip.

The Minister said, 'It's years since I heard from him.
But I've never forgotten him, never. I can show you his
85   photograph in the other room. It's good of him to think of
an old friend. So rich and powerful too. You must ask him
when you go back if he remembers the time —' A bell
began to ring furiously.

Raven thought: the telephone. I cut the wire. It shook
90   his nerve. But it was only the alarm-clock drumming on the
desk. The Minister turned it off. 'One egg's boiled,' he said
and stooped for the saucepan. Raven opened his attaché
case: in the lid he had fixed his automatic fitted with a
silencer. The Minister said: 'I'm sorry the bell made you
95   jump. You see I like my egg just four minutes.'

- What additional information are we given about Raven's attitude to the job?
- How has he reacted to the secretary, and why?

- What do we learn here about the Minister's lifestyle and personality?
- This paragraph seems to hold up the action. What is its purpose?

- How do these two paragraphs help develop or maintain the tension?

- What is the effect of this mixture of the everyday (the egg) and the dramatic (the gun)?

Feet ran along the passage. The door opened. Raven turned furiously in his seat, his hare-lip flushed and raw. It was the secretary. He thought: my God, what a household. They won't let a man do things tidily. He forgot his lip, he was angry, he had a grievance. She came in flashing her gold teeth, prim and ingratiating. She said, 'I was just going out when I heard the telephone,' then she winced slightly, looked the other way, showed a clumsy delicacy before his deformity which he couldn't help noticing. It condemned her. He snatched the automatic out of the case and shot the Minister twice in the back.

Graham Greene: *A Gun for Sale*

- How does Raven react to the secretary's return, and why?

The seeds of action

A novel is not just the narration of a string of events. If it is to make sense to the reader, it must show how the events are linked. The novelist does this, and provides dramatic tension, by sowing the seeds of action.

In the extract you have just read, there is no description of what happens to the secretary, but the writer has left indications that something will happen to her – and the reasons why it must.

1 What are these seeds of action?
2 What do you think will happen to the secretary?
3 What other seeds of action are there in the text?
4 What other actions do you think they might produce?

Writing a critical evaluation

In the text you have been reading, Graham Greene skilfully combines action, atmosphere, character and suspense. Use the notes you have already made to write a critical evaluation of the writer's craft. You should focus on *how* Greene uses language and the effect that it has.

Your response should contain these elements:

- an **introduction** explaining where the extract is from and briefly what it contains

- one or two paragraphs on each of the following:
  action and **tension**
  atmosphere
  character

- a **conclusion** summing up your personal response to the text and the writer's craft.

A22 *The tale and the teller*

Viewpoint

The same story can be told in many different ways. An important choice that a writer makes is of **viewpoint**: the 'angle' from which the story is told. These are some of the possibilities.

1 **First person narration**: the writer takes on the role of the central character and tells the story as if they were that person.
2 **Subjective third person narration**: we see all the events of the story through the eyes of one character and the writer helps us to imagine very fully what is going on in that character's mind.
3 **Objective third person narration**: the writer stands back from the events of the story and describes them as if they were like a god, looking down from above.

There are many transitional stages between 2 and 3. Also a writer may use the subjective third person but shift from one character to another. A further complication is that the writer may enter the story themselves and use the pronoun 'I', but only do so as 'writer' – in other words it is still a third person story, but with personal comments from the writer.

The choice of viewpoint has important effects on the way in which the reader receives the story and reacts to it.

First person

I saw that island first when it was neither night nor morning. The moon was to the west, setting, but still broad and bright. To the east, and right amidships of the dawn, which was all
5 pink, the day-star sparkled like a diamond. The land breeze blew in our faces, and smelt strong of wild lime and vanilla; other things besides, but these were the most plain; and the chill of it set me sneezing. I should say I had been for
10 years on a low island near the line, living for the most part solitary among natives. Here was a fresh experience; even the tongue would be quite strange to me; and the look of these woods and mountains, and the rare smell of
15 them, renewed my blood.

The captain blew out the binnacle lamp.

'There!' said he, 'there goes a bit of smoke, Mr Wiltshire, behind the break of the reef. That's Falesá … '

R.L. Stevenson: *The Beach of Falesá*

the line: the Equator

Subjective third person

Tutti Frutti, the boys called her.

It suited her, somehow; though once you thought about it for a moment it was clearly ridiculous and didn't apply to her in the least. She was totally without frills.

5   He vividly recalled the first time he ever saw her. She was kneeling down on the grass in her back garden, stroking Shakespeare, who had gone through the hole in the fence, exploring. He fell desperately in love with her at once. The time was out of joint: she was sixteen, he was

10   fourteen. He was captivated, transfixed.

     Naturally, he realised, he must have seen her without thinking about it, hundreds – no, thousands of times before. They had always been neighbours, his folks and hers, divided by nothing more than an old wooden paling.

Christopher Rush: *Into the Ebb*

Objective third person

Marley was dead, to begin with. There is no doubt whatever about that. The register of his burial was signed by the clergyman, the clerk, the undertaker, and

5   the chief mourner. Scrooge signed it. And Scrooge's name was good upon 'Change for anything he chose to put his name to.

     Old Marley was as dead as a door-nail.

     Mind! I don't mean to say that I know,

10   of my own knowledge, what there is particularly dead about a door-nail. I might have been inclined, myself, to regard a coffin-nail as the deadest piece of ironmongery in the trade.

Charles Dickens: *A Christmas Carol*

'Change: the Exchange, the place where people did financial deals

The re-write

Either re-write extract **1** in the third person, *or* re-write extract **2** or **3** in the first person. Compare your version with the original. What effects has re-writing it had?

The theft

The extract that follows takes place at the cottage of Silas Marner, a solitary man who has made a great deal of money as a weaver. He has stored all his gold and silver coins in a secret hiding-place in his cottage. Dunstan Cass, the ne'er-do-well son of old Squire Cass, needs money desperately and he decides to visit the weaver and bully him into lending him some. When he reaches the cottage he finds that Silas Marner is not there. He goes inside and looks around.

His eyes travelled eagerly over the floor, where the bricks, distinct in the fire-light, were discernible under the sprinkling of sand. But not everywhere; for there was one spot, and one only, which was quite covered with sand, and sand showing the marks of fingers, which had apparently been careful to spread it over a given space. It was near the treddles of the loom. In an instant Dunstan darted to that spot, swept away the sand with his whip, and, inserting the thin end of the hook between the bricks, found that they were loose. In haste he lifted up two bricks and saw what he had no doubt was the object of his search; for what could there be but money in those two leathern bags? And, from their weight, they must be filled with guineas. Dunstan felt round the hole, to be certain that it held no more; then hastily replaced the bricks, and spread the sand over them. Hardly more than five minutes had passed since he entered the cottage, but it seemed to Dunstan like a long while; and though he was without any distinct recognition of the possibility that Marner might be alive, and might re-enter the cottage at any moment, he felt an undefinable dread laying hold on him, as he rose to his feet with the bags in his hand. He would hasten out into the darkness, and then consider what he should do with the bags. He closed the door behind him immediately, that he might shut in the stream of light: a few steps would be enough to carry him beyond betrayal by the gleams from the shutter-chinks and the latch-hole. The rain and darkness had got thicker, and he was glad of it; though it was awkward walking with both hands filled, so that it was as much as he could do to grasp his whip along with one of the bags. But when he had gone a yard or two he might take his time. So he stepped forward into the darkness.

This is where Chapter 4 ends.

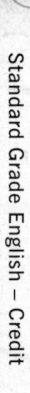

Chapter 5

35   When Dunstan Cass turned his back on the cottage, Silas Marner was not more than a hundred yards away from it, plodding along from the village with a sack thrown round his shoulders as an overcoat, and with a horn-lantern in his hand. His legs were weary, but his mind was at ease …

The author goes on to describe why Silas Marner had left his cottage and why he had failed to lock the door. Silas then begins to get ready for supper …

40   As soon as he was warm he began to think it would be a long while to wait till after supper before he drew out his guineas, and it would be pleasant to see them on the table before him as he ate his unwonted feast. For joy is the best of wine, and Silas's guineas were a wine of that sort.

45   He rose and placed his candle unsuspectingly on the floor near his loom, swept away the sand without noticing any change, and removed the bricks. The sight of the empty hole made his heart leap violently, but the belief that his gold was gone could not come at once – only terror …

George Eliot: *Silas Marner*

Thinking about the viewpoint

1 How would you describe the viewpoint in this extract?
2 Why do you think the writer chose to tell the story in this way?
3 What would be lost if the whole story was told from the viewpoint of Dunstan Cass?
4 What would be lost if the whole story was told from the viewpoint of Silas Marner?

Imaginative writing: Point of view

Think of the outline of a story entitled *The Theft*.

1 Write a list of the main events in the story.
2 Write the names of the main characters.
3 Decide on *two* different viewpoints from which you could tell the story.
4 Write the first three paragraphs of the story from *both* points of view.
5 You now have two versions of the same story. Which is the most interesting and effective? Why?
6 Choose the better version and complete your story.

A23 *What you think ...*

Conversation in literature

When you have a conversation with someone, the words you say often reflect the thoughts that are going on inside your head – or some of them. In stories and plays writers can suggest to us what people are thinking by what they say. If we are going to understand the thoughts of the characters, we often have to do a fair amount of detective work. Sometimes a writer gives us a bit more help.

Countdown

The scene takes place after supper, any evening of any week in any year of this twenty-year-old marriage. (*NOTE*: The dialogue is mainly spoken thoughts. The actual conversation is printed in italics. Stage instructions are printed in italics within brackets.)

HUSBAND: Where's she gone? Making the tea. I haven't heard the whistle. I'll have to get up and carry the tray in when I hear the whistle. I don't know why I ever offered to start carrying the thing in the first place. I've been carrying trays in and out of the door ever since. If they
5   were heavy I'd understand it. I do nothing except walk from here to the kitchen, from the kitchen to here with that tray. It's empty most of the time anyway. Still I suppose it's a nice gesture. At least I do it every day. Not just when we have visitors.
    That tea must be ready by now. Haven't heard the whistle. If she's
10   left the whistle off the kettle it'll be the first time ... (*Rising*) And she talks about me leaving the whistle off. (*He goes out.*)

(Pause. The WIFE enters carrying the tray.)

WIFE: What's happened to him this evening? Must be a world crisis if he's actually forgotten to come padding out to carry this tray. Perhaps he's finally given it up. Thank heavens for that. Forever running in and out with this tray. Why doesn't he behave like a man? I'd like to know what he's done with the whistle off that kettle. Where is he then? *(She begins pouring the tea.)*

(He re-enters.)

HUSBAND: Oh there she is. *(Loudly) Oh there you are, dear.*

WIFE: What does one say to that? *(Loudly) Here I am.*

HUSBAND: *Good.* That's a nasty piece of sarcasm if ever I heard one.

WIFE: *Tea.*

HUSBAND: *Oh, tea! That's nice. (He takes cup from her.)*

WIFE: Surprise, surprise …

HUSBAND: The way she hands me that tea, you'd think it was a cheque for a hundred pounds. I bet she hid that whistle on purpose.

The next few lines

The extract comes from a short play by Alan Ayckbourn. This is how it continues, with the 'thinks' lines removed.

(HUSBAND starts to stir his tea.)

WIFE: It's not sugared.

HUSBAND: Oh no? *(Laughing loudly)* Hey! Do you know what's in the sugar basin … the whistle, the whistle off the kettle!

WIFE: *(Laughing)* Oh really? Fancy. How silly of me.

HUSBAND: Silly you!

(They both laugh gaily at some length.)

Oh dear.

WIFE: Oh dear.

(The HUSBAND laughs at something he's reading. He laughs again. The WIFE laughs suddenly. The HUSBAND folds the newspaper.)

HUSBAND: How's the boiler been today?

WIFE: No trouble at all today.

HUSBAND: Good, must have learnt to behave itself at last, eh?

(He chuckles. She laughs.)

You see, if you keep the air vent unclogged, you're all right.

WIFE: So it said in the instructions.

Alan Ayckbourn: *Countdown*

Filling it out

Look carefully at the way in which Alan Ayckbourn presents the two characters' thoughts in the full script. Think about how those thoughts might develop in this next part of script. For example:

- How long does the wife let the husband go on stirring his tea before telling him there's no sugar in it?
- What is she thinking while he does so?
- What are his thoughts when she does tell him?
- What are the thoughts of each when the whistle from the kettle is found?

Now write your version of this part of the play, including the characters' thoughts spoken aloud.

Elizabeth Gordon Quinn

Author's note

The play is set in Glasgow, 1915.

The Quinn household is squalid. The floor is laid with newspapers. Instead of lifting the newspapers when they get damp and dirty, fresh newspapers are simply laid over the old ones. The most important thing in their small house is a piano which, however, has become a part of the squalor. On top of it are sheet music, unwashed dishes, a Sacred Heart statue, books etc.

The Quinns are of course exotics – their language and their selves are fantastic and extreme. But the **orotundity** of their language is about the energy and imagination required to divert from the actual poverty. This tension is also true of their characters – an element in the grandiose manner of Elizabeth is her personal filth. (I see her as being filthy but presentable!)

Part One, Scene Two

WILLIAM is holding a letter informing him of the forthcoming increases in rent. He is very anxious. ELIZABETH comes in with flowers.

	ELIZABETH:	Hot – it's breathless! I've never known a summer extend itself to this extent.
5	WILLIAM:	Elizabeth.
	ELIZABETH:	I bought some flowers. So refreshing – you could wash your face in them. They're like eager hearts.
	WILLIAM:	We got a letter.
10	ELIZABETH:	Received. 'Got' is not a word. At least not in English. Aren't these lovely?
	WILLIAM:	Rent increases.
	ELIZABETH:	Where will I put them? On top of the piano? Yes. They'll make the whole room resound.
	WILLIAM:	We're in arrears as it is. We're in arrears as it is!
15	ELIZABETH:	Don't be dramatical, William. You're such an amateur.
	WILLIAM:	No. We're not in arrears. I imagined we were but we're not. I was only being dramatical.
	ELIZABETH:	Your voice, William – you are not being strangled.
20	WILLIAM:	I simply want to understand why it has all become so unmanageable. I agree I no longer have a position. I no longer have a position I agree. But that is no reason for us to continue living as if I did! (*Pause. Tentatively.*) Elizabeth.

orotundity – pomposity

	ELIZABETH:	Please do not adopt that tone. You adopt that tone of appeasement when you're about to raise something unpleasant.
25	WILLIAM:	If I adopt a tone, it's because you make it impossible to discuss anything.
	ELIZABETH:	What, for example?
	WILLIAM:	You know what! The piano – the unmentionable.
	ELIZABETH:	We have discussed the piano interminably.
30	WILLIAM:	Discussed, yes.
	ELIZABETH:	Yet you roundly asserted almost in your last sentence that it was impossible for us to discuss anything.
	WILLIAM:	Look at it! It's still here – the animal. Look at the size of it. I don't know how we got it in here.
35	ELIZABETH:	Manoeuvred.
	WILLIAM:	Manoeuvred. I can't describe the panic I feel when I look at it. I look at it and I – completely! – panic.
	ELIZABETH:	Don't look at it then.
	WILLIAM:	Then I think about it even more. I keep expecting it to back into me and stamp on my foot.
40		
	ELIZABETH:	You're a clown, William. Anyone would think you were trying to say something, yet tomorrow you won't remember a thing you've said. If you're saying anything at all you are simply agreeing with me that the house is too small. I don't have room to take a deep breath! In my opinion, what makes everything so unmanageable is that we can't escape from it, with the result we are completely overcrowded!
45		

Chris Hannan: *Elizabeth Gordon Quinn*

Thinking about the situation

In the Author's note, Chris Hannan highlights some key points
relating to setting and character.

1 Read the Author's note again. What are some of the tensions and
contradictions evident in the Quinn household?

2 In this scene, what evidence is there that Elizabeth is not facing
up to 'the actual poverty' of her situation?

3 What do you think William is feeling? How well does he express
his feelings?

4 What do we learn about the couple's relationship?

5 Consider your response to question 1. How has the playwright
conveyed the sense of tension and contradiction present in the
Quinn household?

6 From all the evidence you have, create a character profile
of Elizabeth.

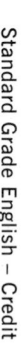

A24 The moon's a balloon ... or is it?

It's a real challenge to describe things in words. Usually people have a good idea about what we are talking about because they have seen something similar. When we are trying to describe a special scene or event, we often end up saying that it is **like** something else. Creative writers do the same thing: when they want to communicate their experience they use comparisons to convey their meaning. When we study literature we look at the way they do it. We also have the chance to consider how well we think they do it.

What's a moon?

– Well, it's round and white.
– Like a mint?
– Not really.
– Like a football?
– Not exactly. It's more like a football than a mint.
– Can you kick it?
– No, stupid, it's in the sky, like a star.
– What's a star?

Brainstorming

■ Think of as many comparisons as you can to describe what the moon is like.
■ Write them down very briefly. Don't worry about the quality, just let your imagination take over.
■ When you have run out of ideas, look back over your list. Try to rank them in order starting with the best and moving downwards.
■ Why do you think some are better than others?

Above the dock

Above the quiet dock in midnight,
Tangled in the tall mast's corded height,
Hangs the moon. What seemed so far away
Is but a child's balloon, forgotten after play.

T.E. Hulme

Like a dying lady

And, like a dying lady lean and pale,
Who totters forth, wrapp'd in a gauzy veil,
Out of her chamber, led by the insane
And feeble wanderings of her fading brain,
5   The moon arose up in the murky east
A white and shapeless mass.

P.B. Shelley

Creating poster poems

These two poems are to be produced by a design studio as full colour posters, combining
the poem with one or more illustrations.

Try writing an **artwork brief** for each one. This is a short but clear description of what
you want an illustrator to do. Its purpose is to ensure that the artists produce the right
kind of illustration which accurately and sympathetically reflects each of the poems.

Figures of speech

Image

A picture created by the words that a poem uses.

In *Above the dock* there is an image of the moon, looking like a balloon caught up in the ship's ropes.

Similes and metaphors are two ways in which images are created.

Simile

A type of image in which one thing is said to be similar to another.

Whilst the word *like* is most often found in a simile, the word *as* is also used.

In *Like a dying lady* the simile is highlighted in the title as well as the poem. The moon is described as being *like* a lady who is dying.

Metaphor

Another type of image. Instead of saying that something is like something else, it is described as if it were actually that thing.

In *Above the dock*, the moon has become the child's balloon which has been left and forgotten.

Personification

Giving human characteristics to animals, plants, ideas or objects.

In *Like a dying lady* the moon is given human characteristics as it is said to totter about the sky like a lady who has lost her mind.

Read the poems and then answer the questions on page 81.

The Gowdan Ba'

The muckle müne noo rows attowre
The humphie-backit brae;
And skimmers doun the Carse o' Gower
And the fluther o' the Tay.

5 O earth, ye've tin'd your gowdan ba';
And yonder, in the nicht,
It birls clean on and far awa
Sae wee and siller-bricht.

William Soutar

Is the moon tired?

Is the moon tired? She looks so pale
    Within her misty veil;
She scales the sky from east to west,
    And takes no rest.

5 Before the coming of the night
    The moon shows papery white;
Before the dawning of the day
    She fades away.

Christina Rossetti

Autumn

A touch of cold in the Autumn night –
I walked abroad,
And saw the ruddy moon lean over a hedge
Like a red-faced farmer.
I did not speak, but nodded,
And round about were the wistful stars
With white faces like town children.

T.E. Hulme

Questions

The Gowdan Ba' and *Is the moon tired?*
1 One of these poems refers to the moon as a person. The other compares it to an object. Why do you think the writers have chosen these approaches?
2 Look at the verbs in *The Gowdan Ba'*. What pictures do they suggest?
3 What are the similarities and differences between the image of the moon in *The Gowdan Ba'* and that presented in *Is the moon tired?*

Autumn
4 What comparisons does T.E. Hulme use for:

■ the moon?
■ the stars?

5 In what ways are they suitable here?

Finding examples

Look again at the poems on these two pages and find examples of each of the figures of speech listed in the box on page 80.

Explaining literary terms

Use the three poems to help you create a straightforward and clear explanation of the words image, simile, metaphor and personification, for a class in the year below yours. How could you check whether they had understood the terms?

A25 Rhyme and rhythm

Literary terms

metre
the rhythm of the line in a poem (the pattern of stressed and unstressed syllables)

iambic
'de-dum', an unstressed syllable followed by a stressed one such as in 'begin'

iambic pentameter
a line with five 'de-dums', a ten-syllable line with the pattern of an unstressed syllable being followed by a stressed one

quatrain
a group of four lines in a poem

stanza
another word for an individual verse in a poem. Used in order to avoid confusion between the idea of a verse in a poem and verse generally.

Rhyme

In playground games, in advertisements, as part of a joke, at a football match, in a song: you can find rhyme in all kinds of places apart from poetry books. But why is it there and what does it do?

> Roses are red,
> Violets are blue,
> Most poems rhyme,
> This one doesn't.

There are plenty of alternative versions of the above poem. Nearly all of them rhyme. When you expect a rhyme and you don't find one, it jars. When you anticipate a rhyme and it occurs, there is a sense that the verse has been completed. The rhyme at the end is sometimes what keeps people reading on. Unusual rhymes can create humour or surprise or both.

> There was a young woman called Maggie
> Whose dog was enormous and shaggy;
> The front end of him
> Looked vicious and grim
> But the tail end was friendly and waggy.

Rhyme schemes

Rhyme schemes are indicated in a fairly straightforward way in poems. The first line is called a and any lines that rhyme with it are also called a . When you come to a line that does not rhyme with it, that gets called b and so do any lines that rhyme with it. This pattern simply continues until the end of the poem.

 a I've got a dog, thin as a rail,
 a He's got fleas all over his tail;
 b Every time his tail goes flop,
 b The fleas on the bottom hop to the top.

To check that you understand this, work out the rhyme scheme for the two previous short poems in this unit.

Thinking

What rhymes can you think of that people might find in places other than a poetry book?

Brainstorm as many as you can remember that are suitable to be repeated in a classroom and try to say where you heard them first.

A rhyme is for ...

Rhymes do all sorts of things. Here are some of the things that other people have claimed that rhymes do.

a Rhymes help to make an idea memorable.
b Rhymes can give a sharpness to what someone is saying.
c Rhymes are the glue that makes words stick together.
d Rhymes help to give a sense of completion.
e Rhymes help to hold a poem together.
f Rhymes help the flow of a poem.
g The pleasure with rhyme is in guessing what comes next.

1 Do you agree with these statements?
2 Put them in order of importance, with the one that best describes what rhymes do at the top.
3 Try explaining why you put the top two in those places.

Rhythm

The effect of a rhyme is often emphasised by a regular rhythm.
It's there in nursery rhymes and playground chants.

> Queenie, Queenie Caroline
> Dipped her hair in turpentine:
> Turpentine to make it shine,
> Queenie, Queenie Caroline.

The pattern here has a stressed (x) sound followed by an unstressed (–) one.

x	–	x	–	x	–	x

Queenie, Queenie Caroline

One of the most common patterns found in English poetry is an unstressed
syllable followed by one that is stressed. It creates a sound pattern that goes
'de dum, de dum, de dum, de dum' for perhaps four or five repetitions in a line.

–	x	–	x	–	x	–	x	–	x

The greatest skill in all the world I hear

–	x	–	x	–	x	–	x	–	x

Is making younger brothers disappear.

Metre

This rhythm of the lines in a poem is called the
metre. The metre in the lines immediately above
is called iambic. The iambic pattern repeats five
times in this case and iambic lines like these are
called **iambic pentameters**.

Of course, very few poems are entirely regular
in their pattern and the exceptions to a pattern are
often part of the interest: they make words and
phrases stand out so that the reader notices them.

Sonnet

One commonly used form in poetry is the sonnet.
This has fourteen lines and a regular rhythmic and
rhyming pattern. The sonnet originated in Italy,
and was first used as a form in which to write a
love poem. However, it has since been used to
write about many other subjects as well.

The first sonnets divided the fourteen lines into
an eight-line verse, followed by a six-line verse.
William Shakespeare developed a new sonnet
form, dividing the fourteen lines into three
quatrains (four-line stanzas), followed by a
couplet. Many sonnets written during the
sixteenth and seventeenth centuries were highly
romantic and idealised about love. By the
twentieth century, poets were using the form for a
very wide range of subjects.

Here are two sonnets by Scottish poets, one written about 1600 and the other written almost four hundred years later. Montgomerie is writing in a highly romantic way to a woman he loves. He suggests that she has stolen away his life, his spirit and his heart. Morgan uses the sonnet form to describe the ugliness and poverty of slum housing. As you read these poems, think about how each poet uses the following features:

- comparisons – are they familiar, or unexpected?
- rhyme scheme – are both poems the same or do they differ?
- quatrains and couplets – how are the poems divided up?
- iambic pentameter – is it used in a regular way throughout both poems?

To His Mistress

So sweet a kiss yestreen frae thee I reft,   **reft:** received
In bowing doun thy body on the bed,
That even my life within thy lips I left.
Sensyne from thee my spirits wald never shed.   **Sensyne:** since then
                                                        shed: be parted
5 To follow thee it from my body fled
And left my corpse als cold as ony key.
But when the danger of my death I dread,
To seek my spreit I sent my hairt to thee;   **spreit:** spirit
But it was so enamoured with thine ee,   **ee:** eye
10 With thee it mindit likewise to remain.   **mindit:** wished
So thou hes keepit captive all the three,
More glaid to bide than to return again.
      Except thy breath their places had suppleit,   **suppleit:** filled, taken over
      Even in thine armes, there doutless had I deit.   **deit:** died

Alexander Montgomerie

A mean wind wanders through the backcourt trash.
Hackles on puddles rise, old mattresses
puff briefly and subside. Play-fortresses
of brick and bric-à-brac spill out some ash.
5 Four storeys have no windows left to smash,
but in the fifth a chipped sill buttresses
mother and daughter, the last mistresses
of that black block condemned to stand, not crash.
Around them, the cracks deepen, the rats crawl.
10 The kettle whimpers on a crazy hob.
Roses of mould grow from ceiling to wall.
The man lies late since he has lost his job,
smokes on one elbow, letting his coughs fall
thinly into an air too poor to rob.

Edwin Morgan, from *Glasgow Sonnets*

A26 Comparisons

Comparing two texts

Students are often required to compare two texts on related topics; it is a common feature of English examination papers. The problems it causes stem largely from the difficulty of talking about two things at the same time: the temptation is to write about one text, then write about the other and finish up with a paragraph or two trying to compare them.

The solution is to look for common themes which will allow you to discuss both texts together, and to build your answer(s) round these. Obviously these themes will vary, but there are certain key things to look for:

Subject matter
- In what ways is the subject matter common to both texts and in what ways does it differ?
- How have the two writers chosen which aspects of the subject to focus on?
- Do they emphasise similar points or different ones?

The writer's voice
- Do we feel the writer's presence strongly in the text, or is the subject matter left to speak for itself?
- Does each writer have a distinctive voice? Are these similar or different? How would you describe them?

Language
- Do the writers use a similar or different vocabulary?
- What use does each make of imagery?
- Is there anything useful to be said about the way each writer constructs sentences? For example, does one writer like long and complicated sentences while the other prefers shorter, simpler ones? What effect does this have?
- Is there a clear rhythm to each writer's sentences?
- What words would you use to sum up the way in which each author writes?

Structure
- How is each text shaped? For example one may have a very clear beginning, middle and end, while the other flows much more freely.

On the next two pages are two texts on the theme of childhood memories.
Read them and then follow the instructions on page 89.

I've been an outsider since the 11-plus

I failed my 11-plus, which was quite a shock as there were only two out of a class of 22 who failed. Everyone had expected me to pass, because my mother made me go to bed early, and that was
5 seen as an indication I must be brainy. There was a massive stigma attached to failing your 11-plus and I remember people being fascinated to discover somebody who had failed, it was like a Martian had landed.

10 I'd had no preparation for the 11-plus, all I knew was you went into a room and took an exam, and if you passed it you went to the grammar school and got a uniform, and could have a good job later on, and if you didn't pass it,
15 you went to Upton Secondary Modern School.

So anyway, the 11-plus day came, it was a steaming hot afternoon, absolutely boiling. We went into the school hall and sat down for three hours, and answered these questions. I'd never sat
20 down for three hours before.

There was only one question I remember: 'What does "quenched" mean?'

Now here I am, 11 years old, my dad works at a pit, my mother is a housewife: we had never used
25 the word 'quenched' in our natural conversation. I had never read a book containing the word 'quenched', I had never seen a film with the word 'quenched' in it, I didn't know what it was. 'Quenched'? 'Quenched'? – it could have been a
30 three-headed monster.

I wanted to play football for Leeds when I was 11, I wasn't interested in anything else; I wanted to be Gary Sprake, the Leeds goalkeeper, and every night I went to bed with my Leeds scarf round my
35 neck.

After about two months, the results came out. A letter dropped through the door. I can still remember my parents reading it and being completely destroyed that I hadn't got into
40 grammar school. My dad lost his temper with frustration and disappointment, and he began shaking me.

The other kids on our estate now had racing bikes, because for some bizarre reason, if you passed your 11-plus you got a racing bike.
45

Naturally I didn't get a racing bike, and I went to the comprehensive, which was really grim. Upton Secondary Modern School. It was secondary and not very modern, about 500 yards from our house.
50

Upton was a mining village, half a mile from the pit, and, of course, most of the lads from the secondary modern went down the pit.

The other boys, the ones who had passed the 11-plus, went to Pontefract Grammar School.
55 Pontefract is only five miles from Upton, but it was an enormous distance; Pontefract was posh, doctors lived in Pontefract, people from Pontefract went to Oxbridge.

Every so often, I'd see the boys of my class
60 who had got into grammar school, and suddenly I realised they were in a different league. Pontefract was *the* school to go to, it was in nice grounds, they had a proper rugby team, and they played rugby union, while we played rugby
65 league. They wore a dark-blue and grey uniform – we didn't have a uniform at Upton Secondary Modern. I sort of yearned for the grammar-school trappings, and yet I despised them at the same time.

Later, I went to train as a teacher, and these
70 grammar-school guys were doing degrees in economics, and science, and so they would continue making you feel small, insecure …

The only good thing I can say about the 11-plus is I did a degree, and then I did a Masters degree,
75 and I did a five-year PhD, and then I was given an honorary PhD. I don't think I would have sought all that so much if I'd passed my bloody 11-plus.

I'm actually still coming to terms with it now, and even though I've got accolades and degrees
80 and awards for my work, quite honestly, I still feel I'm on the outside of the theatre fraternity, I don't belong to it at all. And I know it was the 11-plus which helped me feel like an outsider.

John Godber in conversation with Dannie Danziger

The Independent, 21 March 1994

Whipped with branches

I still remember – my hands and finger tips still remember! – what used to lie in store for us on our return to school from the holidays. The guava trees in the schoolyard would be in full leaf
5 again, and the old leaves would be strewn around in scattered heaps. In places there were even more than just heaps of them: it would be like a muddy sea of leaves.

'Get that all swept up!' the headmaster would
10 tell us. 'I want the whole place cleaned up, at once!'

'At once!' There was enough work there, damned hard work, too, to last us for over a week. Especially since the only tools with which
15 we were provided were our hands, our fingers, our nails.

'Now see it's done properly, and be quick about it,' the headmaster would say to the older pupils, 'or you'll have to answer for it!'
20 So at an order from the older boys we would all line up like peasants about to reap or glean a field, and we would set to work like members of a chain-gang. In the schoolyard itself it wasn't too bad: the guava trees were fairly well spaced; but
25 there was one part where the closely-planted trees grew in a hopeless tangle of leaves and branches. The sun could not penetrate here, and the acrid stench of decay lingered in the undergrowth even at the height of summer.

If the work was not going as quickly as the 30 headmaster expected, the big boys, instead of giving us a helping hand, used to find it simpler to whip us with branches pulled from the trees. Now guava wood is regrettably flexible; skilfully handled, the springy switches used to whistle 35 piercingly, and fall like flails of fire on our backsides. Our flesh stung and smarted, while tears of anguish sprang from our eyes and splashed on the rotting leaves at our feet.

Occasionally, one of us, worn out by such 40 calculated cruelty, would have the courage to complain to the headmaster. He would of course be very angry, but the punishment he inflicted on the older boys was always negligible – nothing compared to what they had done to us. And the 45 fact is that however much we complained, our situation did not improve in the slightest. Perhaps we should have let our parents know what was going on, but somehow we never dreamed of doing so; I don't know whether it was loyalty or 50 pride that kept us silent, but I can see now that we were foolish to keep quiet about it for such beatings were utterly foreign to our nature, to the most fundamental and secret principles of our character, and completely at variance with our 55 passion for independence and equality.

Camara Laye

Collecting evidence

The first thing to do is to make sure that you have a good – and detailed –
grasp of both texts.

1 Take a large sheet of paper and draw up a table like the one below.
2 Read both texts again and fill in as much information as you can. Put in
  line references so that you can find things easily.

	John Godber		Camara Laye	
	Comment	Line(s)	Comment	Line(s)
Subject matter				
The writer's voice				
Language				
Structure				

Answering questions

Use the material you have collected to help you answer these
questions. Write your answers in the form of complete sentences.

1 What do you learn from the two passages about what schools were
  like in the different cultures which are described?
2 What picture do you have from each text about the society in
  which each lived?
3 What impressions have you gained of the personalities of John
  Godber and Camara Laye? Do they have anything in common?
4 What evidence is there in the two texts that they have reflected
  upon the experiences they describe? What conclusions, if any, does
  each draw about the importance of the experience in his life?

Writing a comparison

Choose one of these topics and write about it.

1 What are the similarities and differences in the childhood
  experiences described by John Godber and Camara Laye?
2 'Childhood experiences have much in common throughout the
  world and across history.' Do these two texts make you want to
  agree or disagree with this point of view?

Section B contents

....

Each unit in this section focuses on a specific area of your syllabus: poetry, prose (pre- and post-1900), drama, media and non-fiction. The units offer opportunities to develop the skills from section A, practise for exams and undertake coursework assignments.

Activities are categorised like this:

Preparation The reading, thinking and note-making required before undertaking longer pieces of writing or talking in response to a text, topic or situation.

Practice Activities which result in a 'product' – usually, but not always, an extended piece of writing. These can be used for exam practice.

Coursework Longer writing activities which can produce material suitable for inclusion in a coursework folder.

B1 Fiction
STONE COLD

See:
- **A20** Character (p62)
- **A21** Action (p66)
- **A22** Viewpoint (p70)

Link is a homeless teenager living down and out in London. He describes what it is really like to live rough in such vivid detail it is easy for us to feel sorry for him.

So you pick your spot. Wherever it is (unless you're in a squat or a derelict house or something) it's going to have a floor of stone, tile, concrete or brick. In
5 other words it's going to be hard and cold. It might be a bit cramped too – shop doorways often are. And remember, if it's winter you're going to be half frozen before you even start.
10 Anyway you've got your place, and if you're lucky enough to have a sleeping-bag you unroll it and get in.

15 Settled for the night? Well maybe, maybe not. Remember my first night? The Scouser? 'Course you do. He kicked me out of my bedroom and pinched my watch. Well, that sort of thing can happen any night, and there are worse things. You could be peed on by a drunk or a dog. Happens all the time – one man's bedroom is another man's lavatory. You might be spotted by a gang of lager louts on the look-out for someone to maim. That happens all the time too, and if they get carried away you can end up dead. There are guys who like young boys, who think because you're a dosser you'll do anything for dosh, and there's the psycho
20 who'll knife you for your pack.

So you lie listening. You bet you do. Footsteps. Voices. Breathing, even. Doesn't help you sleep.

Then there's your bruises. What bruises? Try lying on a stone floor for half an hour. Just half an hour. You choose any position you fancy, and you won't find it comfy, I can tell you.
25 You won't sleep unless you're dead drunk or zonked on downers. And if you are, and do, you're going to wake up with bruises on hips, shoulders, elbows, ankles, and knees – especially if you're a bit thin from not eating properly. And if you do that for six nights you'll feel like you fell out of a train. Try sleeping on concrete then.

And don't forget the cold. If you've ever tried dropping off to sleep with cold feet, even in
30 bed you'll know it's impossible. You've got to warm up those feet, or lie awake. And in January, in a doorway, in wet trainers, it can be quite a struggle. And if you manage it, chances are you'll need to get up for a pee, and then it starts all over again.

And those are only some of the hassles. I haven't mentioned stomach cramps from hunger, headaches from the flu, toothache, fleas and lice. I haven't talked about homesickness,
35 depression or despair. I haven't gone into how it feels to want a girlfriend when your circumstances make it virtually impossible for you to get one – how it feels to know you're a social outcast in fact, a non-person to whom every ordinary everyday activity is closed.

Robert Swindells: *Stone Cold*

Preparation

Thinking points

As you look at the passage again carefully, try to work out how the writer makes us feel sorry for Link. You need to look at the details.

1 Make a list of the facts Link tells us about sleeping on concrete.
2 What dangers does he face? Are they written in any particular order?
3 Why do you think Link mentions all the things 'I haven't mentioned'?
   What different areas of life do they cover?
4 Which of the following words do you think best describes Link's mood or attitude?

   sad   matter of fact   angry   cheerful
   confident   worried   calm

   Now pick out three or four phrases that prove your answer is right.

5 How does the writer make it seem as if Link is speaking directly to you as someone who will understand?
   Pick out five words or phrases and try to explain how they have this effect.

Shelter

Not everyone feels so kindly towards the homeless. A man called Shelter believes he is doing a service to his country by killing teenage street people.

Three is a significant number. It crops up in all sorts of places. Three cheers. The Three Musketeers. If I had three wishes. Three blind mice. The Blessed Trinity. The three armed services. The three little pigs. A significant number.

5   I have three recruits now. When I had one I was a murderer, two, a double murderer, and now that I've got three I suppose I'm a mass murderer – what the Yanks call a serial killer. If they caught me now, which they won't, they'd probably make a film of me.

   Naturally, I've arranged them in the Army way – tallest on the

10 left, shortest on the right and they look quite smart – especially now that I've cut their hair. I'll have to try to get them some boots, or at least proper shoes – something which will take a shine. At the moment they're all wearing those manky trainer things.

   Last night's bit of business – signing up recruit number three –

15 gave me particular pleasure. You'll know why presently, but let me start at the beginning. It was about 20.00 hours and I'd just begun my nightly patrol. It was an unpleasant evening – wind and sleet – exactly the sort of evening one needs in my line of work …

Robert Swindells: *Stone Cold*

Preparation

Thinking points

- Is Shelter mad?
- Is Shelter evil?
- What do you think and what are your reasons?

Remember to look at the details.

Studying the characters

Make up a table comparing Link and Shelter. Set it out like the one below.

	What we learn	Where/how we learn it
Facts (age, gender, background, etc.)		
Personality		
Current lifestyle		
Past experiences		
Attitude to self		
Attitude to other people		

Living rough

An advertisement is going to be made using the character of Link to warn teenagers against running away from home and telling them of some of the horrors they might face living rough in a big city.

You are the director. What advice would you give to an actor who has read the passages you have read and is preparing to play the part of Link? Think about these points:

- What is Link like?
- How does Link make the reader feel that he is a friend?
- How does Link make the dangers he faces vivid?

Think of examples from the text to back up your ideas. You should find that the answers you made to the earlier questions will help you. Write the text of what you would say to the actor.

Crimewatch

You are the police officer investigating the serial killer who calls himself Shelter. You are appearing on *Crimewatch* to appeal to the public for help in tracking this man down.

You have found the three bodies mentioned and the page from Shelter's diary (which you can refer to when making your appeal).

What can you tell the public about the man you are looking for? Write your answer as a single speech or as a script in which you are being interviewed about the case.

Commentary

Write a commentary on the extracts you have read. You should include comments on:

- the theme
- the two characters and the way in which they are presented
- the writer's use of viewpoint
- the atmosphere.

Make sure that you support each point you make by reference to the text.

B2 NIGHTMARE... or *dream?*

See: ● **A4** Reading in detail (p13)
● **A5** Reading 'between the lines' (p17) ● **A26** Comparisons (p86)

When steam trains first appeared in the early nineteenth century, they were often greeted with a mixture of fear and awe. Travellers who had been used to stage coaches were amazed at the speeds possible, but were unsure about safety. One of the earliest accounts of a passenger journey by rail is in a letter written by Charles Young to his sister, Jane, in August 1835. Charles had travelled from Yorkshire to Castletown in the Isle of Man, and part of his journey had been on the Manchester to Liverpool railway.

A 6 found all of us in our omnibus on our way to the much talked of railhead. On reaching this office, as soon as you have paid your fare, you are commanded to walk upstairs to the coach rooms – this movement is just like going up
5 the stairs of Queen's Street Chapel.

    Reaching the top, there you behold a range of coaches of large dimension fastened close to each other. Some are closed like our Leeds coach, and others are open on the sides – in order to have a view of the country, as I thought,
10 and of their manner of proceeding. We all took our place in an open one, which resembles an omnibus. Before starting, I took a survey of all around, first placing my little ones safe. The steam carriage which propels each train is something like a distilling wagon and have each a name
15 of no inviting character, for instance, Fury, Victory, Rapid, Vulcan, Tiger and so on.

railhead: station at end of line

distilling wagon: machine for making alcoholic drinks
Vulcan: ancient Roman god of fire

A FIRST-CLASS TRAIN ON THE LIVERPOOL AND MANCHESTER RAIL-WAY. 1833.

20

25

A few minutes after 7 we started, not very fast at first, but, in less than five minutes, off we went like a shot from a gun. No sooner did we come to a field than it was a mile behind us, but this was nothing in comparison with meeting a long train of carriages from Liverpool. I was never so frighted in my life than at this moment; I shrank back completely horrified in my seat; I do not think the train was more than 2 seconds in passing, yet it was as long as Holywell Hill. We were then going at a full 34 miles an hour, consequently they passed us at double that time.

30

35

It is impossible to form any idea of the rapidity of moving. Several other trains passed us, but as I was aware of their approach they no longer alarmed me as at first. The first 17 miles we went in 32 minutes. I am much disappointed in the view of the country, the railway being cut through so many hills you have frequently for miles only clay mounds on each side of you – consequently no splendid prospect can attract your attention. Even when the railway is on a bridge or at an elevation above the usual track of land, you are not charmed by that diversity of prospect which is to be met with in ordinary stage coach travelling. That has a decided superiority over this new work of man.

diversity of prospect: variety of view

40

I was an hour and a quarter going the 33 miles, the latter part of the journey being performed at the slow speed of 20 miles an hour. Previous to entering Liverpool, you go through a dark, black, ugly, vile, abominable tunnel of 300 yards long, which has all the horrors of banishment from life – such a hole as I never wish to go through again, unless my time is as precious as it was the other day.

Charles Young

Preparation

Write short answers to these questions. Make a note of line numbers of sections which back up your answers. You will need to refer to this material later on.

First thoughts

1 What aspects of railway travel frightened Charles?
2 What aspects disappointed him?

Overview

3 How would you sum up his overall feeling towards steam trains?

Close reading

4 Suppose you were alive in 1835 and had never seen, or travelled on, a train. If you had received Charles' letter, what factual knowledge would you have gained about this new form of transport?

A SECOND-CLASS TRAIN ON THE LIVERPOOL AND MANCHESTER RAIL-WAY. 1833.

Standard Grade English – Credit

Nowadays, most travellers take railways for granted and even regard them as a slow or inconvenient way of travelling compared with cars or planes. In the following extract from her autobiography *Off the Rails*, Lisa St Aubin de Teran presents a different view, however.

B I first discovered trains as a means of truancy, and thus they have remained, irrevocably linked in my mind with the idea of escape. They are the vehicles of romance and adventure, a lifeline promising relief from dullness. I have woven a network of fantasy around the very concept of the train, so wide

5 that the actuality of the journey can rarely outweigh the overall sense of glamour and daring which rail-travel has in my head. Myths begin naturally and then are moulded and sculptured and treasured until they grow out of all proportion to the initial grain of truth. My own love of the railways hovers now somewhere between the improbable and the insane. Sometimes, as I

10 squeeze my way through grime and empty beer cans, past over-stressed commuters or over-wrought shoppers or over-sexed hikers, and the trains are late and the loos blocked and the buffet closed, I stand in wonder at the lengths to which I will go to foster my dream. This dream is of travel and romance, and of romantic travel. I have spent years in seemingly purposeless

15 drifting, but I believe that when I search it is for a moment when time stands still – the pause in the ballet leap, the volatile thrill of perfection. Travelling is like flirting with life. It's like saying 'I would stay and love you, but I have to go; this is my station.' For the rootless and the restless, and the just plain curious, it is a way of being inside the kaleidoscope, but with a way out and a

20 flexible timetable.

Many a one before me has stirred to great railway journeys. But when I say I love trains, I mean I love them all. Not just the wild and wonderful ones, but the ones that go from Liverpool Street to King's Lynn and Colchester, and the ones from Paddington to Bristol Temple Meads, the night trains and the

25 day trains and even the little shuttles from Waterloo to Kingston-upon-Thames and others of that ilk. Brighton was my first dream to come true, and the train journey there my first taste of this recurring magic.

Lisa St Aubin de Teran: *Off the Rails*

irrevocably: unchangingly, for ever

volatile: lively but short-lived

kaleidoscope: tube containing coloured pieces of glass which produce constantly changing patterns when turned and viewed through eyepiece

of that ilk: like that
recurring: constantly remembered

Preparation

Write short answers to these questions. Make a note of line numbers of sections which back up your answers. You will need to refer to this material later on.

First thoughts

5 Why is Lisa excited by travelling on trains?

6 Why is she surprised that they have this effect on her?

Overview

7 What sort of person do you think Lisa is from the evidence of this passage?

Close reading

8 Imagine you are researching a school project about different ways of travelling. What use could you make of this text to argue that trains are not an ideal method of passenger transport?

Practice

Comparisons

1 Both writers express vividly their thoughts and feelings about railway travel. In what ways are their responses similar and what ways are they different?

2 Look again at the language and references to everyday life in both passages. Write between 100 and 150 words about contrasts between the two passages which make it obvious that passage **A** was written almost 150 years before passage **B**.

Points to think about:

■ references to things (for example 'distilling wagon' in **A**)
■ the words used
■ the way in which the writers construct their sentences.

Your writing

Choose one of the following to write about.

1 You have been one of the first travellers to use a new form of transport. Write a letter to a friend describing your experience. You should:

■ decide whether you are writing about a form of transport which already exists (such as an aeroplane), or whether you are going to imagine something completely new
■ include both factual information which you think will interest your friend, and a vivid description of your feelings.

2 Use this sentence as the opening of a story:

'Brighton was my first dream to come true, and the train journey there my first taste of this recurring magic.'

You should:

■ think carefully about who you are, what your dream was, and what this recurring magic is
■ try to create a particular mood in your readers by a careful choice of words in your descriptive writing.

B3 KELLY WOOD

See: ● **A5** Reading 'between the lines' (p17) ● **A24** Metaphor (p80)

Walking in Kelly Wood, gathering words
Frail as spilt leaves, fine sticks of sentences,
Spirals of bracken from the fallen ground,
I listen for the silences of stone,
5 The stream's white voice, the indifference of birds.
Safe in my quiet house I lay them out
– Leaf, stick and bracken – in the hearth's cold frame,
Strike steel on flint against the page of dark,
Wait patiently for the first spark. A flame.

Charles Causley

Preparation

So that's a poem, so what?

It's often easier to talk and write about stories and novels than it is about poems: there are more words to discuss. With a story, you can always fall back on describing what happened (even when you've been warned again and again not to re-tell the story!).

With a poem you are often asking yourself the six key questions in the box.

Of course, it's not as simple as working through a list of questions. Look below at how these general questions become thoughts and further questions about Kelly Wood.

Key questions

1 What is the poem saying to me?
2 Why was it written in this way?
3 What is unusual about the poem?
4 What is distinctive about the way words are used?
5 What impression do I get from the poem as a whole?
6 What do I feel about the poem?

Why gather words in a <u>wood</u>?

words – leaves
sticks – sentences
bracken – ???

No good?
Too feeble?
Why frail?

Walking in Kelly Wood, gathering words
Frail as spilt leaves, fine sticks of sentences,
Spirals of bracken from the fallen ground,
I listen for the silences of stone,
The stream's white voice, the indifference of birds.
Safe in my quiet house I lay them out
– Leaf, stick and bracken – in the hearth's cold frame,
Strike steel on flint against the page of dark,
Wait patiently for the first spark. A flame.

How can you
<u>listen</u> to silence?

Why white?
What sort
of voice?

Not caring?
Just background
noise?

dark=no words?
no ideas?
no use for words?

Doesn't happen
in a minute

Which could be ...?

Good pic. of getting idea for writing
– like the sense of gathering
– like the idea that it takes time to do it properly

Practice

Coming to a sense of the poem

The notes around the poem show some clear responses to what Charles Causley has written. There are still a lot of questions and uncertainties. How many of those areas can you shed light on or offer further thoughts for?

1 Think about these responses and then write at least one sentence in answer to each of the Key questions.
2 Look at what you have written and then organise your thoughts into a paragraph describing your response to the poem.

Roadgang Women

As you read this second poem, think about
these five basic questions:

- What is happening?
- Where is it happening?
- When is it happening?
- Who is involved?
- Why might they be behaving as they are?

Here come the stonebreakers,
these little skeletons of the roadgang women
with their long strands of hair
knotted high at the back of their skulls.

5   They take a moment
to wipe sweat from around their eyes
with a corner of torn sari.
The road waits for their hands.

They carry stones in baskets on their heads,
10   like apricots marked by a bird's beak,
wizened and bruised:
both heads and stones.

A raised track on a country without limit.
A big sun beating off any shade.
15   A woman stitches a piece of shadow
with an upright stick and sacking.

She breaks stones below it.
Once, she eats from a shallow tin dish
with not much in it;
20   some steamed riceflour cake.

Old women of thirty
work in the day's quickforge.
Nobody can work like them,
though they pause to quarrel or laugh.

25   They must find fire nourishing,
as the salamander does, who is meant
to live in the flames,
where others would die, she lives happily.

Valerie Gillies

Practice

Working through the poem in more detail

1 Describe the scene in the poem in your own words.
2 How does the narrator in the poem feel about the roadgang women?
3 What features of the poem give you evidence of the narrator's feelings?
4 In the poem, a number of comparisons are used (similes and metaphors).
   Choose two examples which you find effective and comment on them in any way you can.
5 List all the ways in which the poet makes reference to the heat of the day.
   Comment on the overall effect of these references.
6 Comment on the image of the salamander in the final stanza. What effect does this image achieve?
7 What effect does the absence of rhyme have on the poem?

Thinking about the poem as a whole

Look at the following statements about the poem.
Which ones describe the poem best?

Put the statements in order, starting with the best.
Explain why you chose this order.

a The poem suggests that the women display endurance.
b The poem deplores the fact that women should have to do such work.
c The poem celebrates the ability to endure.
d The poem dwells on the harshness of the women's working environment.
e The poem implies that the women are not unhappy in what they do.
f The poem gives a picture of an unfamiliar culture.

Practice

Coursework

Extended response to reading: critical evaluation

Sometimes a poem creates a very powerful picture of a place or experience that is unfamiliar to the reader.

Write a critical evaluation of *The Roadgang Women*, using the thoughts and ideas you have been developing in response to the above statement. The Key questions on page 101 may also help you to develop your response further, but do not simply answer those questions.

To help you to organise your critical evaluation, here are some steps to follow:

1 Introduce the poem in relation to the question.
2 Identify key aspects of the poem which relate to the question, and discuss each of these in detail, making use of quotation, critical terms and your own personal responses.
3 Conclude with a summing up, where you comment on the poem as a whole.

B4 The *blind* man

See: ● **A5** Reading 'between the lines' (p17) ● **A20** Character (p62) ● **A13** Narrative (p39)

Kate Chopin lived in St Louis in the southern part of the United States during the latter half of the nineteenth century. After her husband died in 1882, she lived an independent and sometimes controversial life, making a living partly as a writer. Although society was showing signs of change, her friendships with married men were frowned upon and her novel which painted a negative picture of marriage was described as 'poison'.

Kate Chopin wrote the short story *The Blind Man* in the summer of 1896 and it was published in *Vogue* in May of the following year. In those days, *Vogue* was a young progressive magazine that was willing to publish stories about the world as it really was, rather than a romantic version of that world.

Everyday life in St Louis in the 1890s was not easy. Industrial growth had brought rapid change. For example, the arrival of electricity meant that great tram cars could cover the length and breadth of the city. This increasing success of industry meant wealth for some people. It also meant poverty for many others. The gap between rich and poor was widening and there was a sense of unrest which led to a growing number of strikes.

The last decade of the century was also a time of uncertainty for those who had money. A series of panics swept through financial markets wiping out the value of some people's investments. The most dramatic changes in society were still to come but the tensions that existed meant that no one could feel safe from change. The old world was not yet breaking apart, but the cracks were showing.

A man carrying a small red box in one hand walked slowly down the street. His old straw hat and faded garments looked as if the rain had
5 often beaten upon them, and the sun had as many times dried them upon his person. He was not old, but he seemed feeble; and he walked in the sun, along the blistering asphalt
10 pavement. On the opposite side of the street there were trees that threw a thick and pleasant shade; people were all walking on that side. But the man did not know, for he was blind,
15 and moreover he was stupid.

In the red box were lead pencils, which he was endeavouring to sell. He carried no stick, but guided himself by trailing his foot along the stone copings or his hand along the iron railings. When he came to the steps of a house he would mount them. Sometimes, after reaching the
20 door with great difficulty, he could not find the electric button, whereupon he would patiently descend and go his way. Some of the iron gates were locked – their owners being away for the summer – and he would consume much time in striving to open them, which made little difference, as he had all the time there was at his disposal.

25 At times he succeeded in finding the electric button; but the man or maid who answered the bell needed no pencil, nor could they be induced to disturb the mistress of the house about so small a thing.

The man had been out long and had walked very far, but had sold nothing. That morning someone who had finally grown tired of having
30 him hanging around had equipped him with this box of pencils, and sent him out to make his living. Hunger, with sharp fangs, was gnawing at his stomach and a consuming thirst parched his mouth and tortured him. The sun was broiling. He wore too much clothing – a vest and coat over his shirt. He might have removed these and carried
35 them on his arm or thrown them away; but he did not think of it. A kind-hearted woman who saw him from an upper window felt sorry for him, and wished that he would cross over into the shade.

The man drifted into a side street, where there was a group of noisy, excited children at play. The colour of the box which he carried
40 attracted them and they wanted to know what was in it. One of them attempted to take it away from him. With the instinct to protect his own and his only means of sustenance, he resisted, shouted at the children and called them names. A policeman coming around the corner and seeing that he was the centre of a disturbance, jerked him
45 violently around by the collar; but upon perceiving that he was blind, considerately refrained from clubbing him and sent him on his way. He walked on in the sun.

stone copings: kerbstones

broiling: burning (literally cooking on an open flame)

vest: waistcoat

sustenance: making a living

During his aimless rambling he turned into a street where there were monster electric cars thundering up and down, clanging wild
50 bells and literally shaking the ground beneath his feet with their terrific impetus. He started to cross the street.

Then something happened – something horrible happened that made the women faint and the strongest men who saw it grow sick and dizzy. The motorman's lips were as gray as his face, and that was
55 ashen gray; and he shook and staggered from the superhuman effort he had put forth to stop his car.

Where could the crowds have come from so suddenly, as if by magic? Boys on the run, men and women tearing up on their wheels to see the sickening sight; doctors dashing up in buggies as if directed by
60 Providence.

And the horror grew when the multitude recognized in the dead and mangled figure one of the wealthiest, most useful and most influential men of the town – a man noted for his prudence and foresight. How could such a terrible fate have overtaken him? He was
65 hastening from his business house – for he was late – to join his family, who were to start in an hour or two for their summer home on the Atlantic coast. In his hurry he did not perceive the other car coming from the opposite direction, and the common, harrowing thing was repeated.
70 The blind man did not know what the commotion was all about. He had crossed the street, and there he was, stumbling on in the sun, trailing his foot along the coping.

Kate Chopin

buggies: small horse-drawn carriages

prudence: caution, carefulness

Preparation

Initial impressions

1 On pages 105 and 106 the illustrator has offered two pictures of the blind man. Which one do you think is more accurate and why?
2 How would you describe the blind man so that an artist could produce the best possible illustration?

Reading about a life

How do you know what kind of life was experienced by the blind man? Look at the story paragraph by paragraph.
What things give you an impression of what his life was like?

1 Pick out the important phrases about the blind man's life and explain what you think you learn from them. It could start like this:

'old straw hat' and 'faded' clothes suggest he is poor

2 From your notes, write a description in your own words of what life was like for the blind man.
3 Compare your view of the blind man which has grown out of looking at the story in detail, with your initial impression. How has your view changed?
4 Do you think that Kate Chopin is sympathetic or unsympathetic in her portrayal of the blind man? Or is she neither of those things? What are the reasons for your response?

Practice

Life in the 1890s

Look back at the introduction to the story on page 104 which tells you something about society at the time Kate Chopin was writing. It was a world in which people were experiencing:

■ the growth of industrial towns
■ tensions between rich and poor
■ worries about money and security
■ concerns about how people were behaving
■ concerns about the way society was working.

In what ways are these things reflected in this short story? Here is one thought in note form to get you started:

• blind man trying to scratch a living by selling pencils
• big houses have servants 'man or maid'
• they do not want to disturb the 'mistress of the house'
• some iron gates locked – people 'away for the summer'
• rich/poor divide
• locked gate is a physical barrier
• maid is a human barrier
• poverty kept out of contact with wealth.

Make your own notes on this and then use them to write an account of how the story reflects the changes that were taking place in society at the time it was written.

Your own story

Write a story about an outsider in which something unexpected happens.

1 Think about the kind of outsider you might write about:

■ someone with a disability – if so, what disability?
■ someone who looks different – how?
■ someone who thinks differently – in what ways?

2 Think about what might happen in your story:

■ will it be an incident – what sort?
■ will it be a slice of their normal life?
■ what twist or surprise could there be?

3 Think about how your story might challenge people's prejudices.
4 Write your story.

Standard Grade English – Credit

B5 *YOUNG PEOPLE AND DRINKING*

See:
- **A2** Finding things (p8)
- **A4** Reading for detail (p13)
- **A15** Explanation (p46)
- **A16** Argument and persuasion (p49)

Teenage crime surge drink-related

New figures on vandalism and violence

Town centre ban 'huge success'

Proposal for alcohol-free streets countrywide

Young drinkers want 'high kick and quick buzz'

The 18-24 market consumes less but wants premium strength

YOUNG
PEOPLE
AND
DRINKING

A GUIDE FOR PARENTS

The main text in this unit is a leaflet for parents, suggesting ways in which they can advise teenage sons and daughters about alcohol.

On each page there are questions about the contents of the leaflet and your response to it, which you should *discuss in groups* before reading the next section.

As you will be expected to share your group's views with the rest of the class, *you should make brief notes* on the main points of your discussion at each point.

The notes you make will help you prepare for the final written task.

INTRODUCTION

Being a parent can be rewarding and fulfilling. It can also be frustrating and, on occasions, painful.

5 An important responsibility of parents is to prepare their children to cope with the adult world.

Children have much to learn and they begin learning from a very early age. Schools play a large role. Friends and relatives are important.

10 But, usually, it is parents who have the most important influence on their children.

To discuss some subjects with their children can be difficult for parents. Sex is one and illicit drugs is another. Yet another is to do with drink-

15 ing alcohol.

This is a guide to help you help your children to make sensible decisions about drinking and, if they choose to drink, to do so responsibly.

SETTING AN EXAMPLE

This pamphlet will help you to have sensible discussions with your children about drinking. 20

But remember, how much you drink and how you behave will have a big influence on them. For instance, do you set a good example to your children about drinking and driving? You cannot expect them to respect you if you say one thing 25 and then do another.

Talk to your children about drinking when you get the chance but don't try to frighten them with scare stories. Children are very sharp and quick to spot exaggerations – especially when 30 they might not want to believe them.

So be factual – your children will be better equipped to make sensible decisions about drinking if they know the facts.

Preparation

Questions

1 Do you agree that 'usually, it is parents who have the most important influence on their children'?
2 Do you agree that parents can find it difficult to discuss drinking alcohol with their children? Why / Why not?
3 What picture do you have of the way the writer regards families?
4 What picture do you have of the way the writer regards young people?

BASIC FACTS

35 **Fact 1** In whatever form you drink it, alcohol has the same effect on your body.

Fact 2 Those who think that they will come to no harm if they avoid spirits or that beers and ciders are always the weakest 40 alcoholic drinks are quite wrong.

Fact 3 A useful way of knowing how much alcohol you are drinking is to think in terms of units. 1 unit means a $^1/_2$ pint of standard beer or cider or 1 pub tot 45 of spirits or $^3/_4$ of a glass of wine or 1 pub measure of fortified wine (sherry, port etc.). So the drinks illustrated below contain roughly the same amount of alcohol.

2 units = 2 units = 2 units = 2 units

50 **Fact 4** Different brands of an alcoholic drink may be quite different in strength. A strong beer or cider is sometimes twice as strong as the standard product.

440ml = 2 pints Standard beer or cider

Fact 5 All drinks have their strength shown 55 on the label. This is indicated as a percentage (%) by volume and may appear as Alcohol x% vol, Alc x% vol or x% where x shows the actual percentage of alcohol in the container.

Fact 6 It is illegal to drink alcoholic drinks on 60 licensed premises or buy them from an off-licence if you are under 18 years old. Beer may be taken in a pub with a meal if you are over 16 years old.

Fact 7 Despite this, research shows that 30% 65 of young people between 16 and 18 drink regularly on licensed premises.

Fact 8 For a young person to pretend to be 18 isn't clever – this could result in the licensee losing his or her licence and 70 livelihood.

Fact 9 Research shows that 44% of young people between 16 and 18 years have experienced hangovers.

Fact 10 The body burns up alcohol at the rate 75 of 1 unit an hour (see Fact 3). No amount of exercise, fresh air, black coffee or 'quack' medicines can speed this up.

Fact 11 Driving skills are badly affected by 80 alcohol – young people's more than adults'. The most sensible option if you are going to drive is not to drink.

Preparation

Questions

Facts 1–11

5 Which of these facts did you know already?
6 Did any of them come as a surprise to you?
7 Did you find any of them difficult to understand?
8 In what ways (if any) do you think knowing these facts would be likely to change people's attitudes and behaviour?

IN THE HOME

Here are some simple, but very important,
85 home rules:-

- If you drink in the home always stay in control – make it a natural and enjoyable part of your lifestyle;

- Don't encourage your children to drink - if
90 they want a taste of what you are drinking, give them a sip but don't make a big issue out of it. Remember it is illegal to give alcohol to a child under 5 years old;

- Never let teenagers drink in your home unless
95 a responsible adult is present. An unsupervised party is asking for trouble – make sure plenty of non-alcoholic drinks are available;

- Don't leave alcohol lying around – keep it in a secure cupboard or drinking cabinet;

100 - Give your children the facts about alcohol and drinking. Be natural and open. Don't preach or moralise. There is no ideal age to begin giving information and advice but it should be before the teenage years;

- Stay up and greet your child when he or she 105 comes home – this makes it obvious that you are concerned – take an interest in where they are going or where they have been.

COPING WITH TROUBLE

If your teenage son or daughter comes home drunk don't overreact but use this as an opportu- 110 nity, when he or she is over it, to have a straight talk. Don't preach or moralise - be calm and reasonable.

THE MAIN AIM

Always try to help your children to make sensible decisions about drinking. This means, if 115 they choose to drink, respecting the law and always staying in control. Try to prevent drinking problems before they occur.

The Portman Group:
Young People and Drinking

Standard Grade English – Credit

Preparation

Activities

9 Do you think the advice given here is helpful to parents?

10 If they follow it, do you think it will work?

11 On this page the words 'Don't preach or moralise' are used twice. What do they mean?

12 Why do you think this advice is repeated in this way?

Assessment

Work in a small group.

1 Look again carefully at these sections:

- Coping with trouble
- The main aim.

2 Choose one of these sections and look at it again:

- Introduction
- Setting an example
- Basic facts 1–5
- Basic facts 6–11
- In the home.

3 Bearing in mind that this is a leaflet for parents, consider:

- Which points do you think are particularly good, and/or particularly well presented?
- Could some of the points be presented in a better way?
- Do you think that there are other points to make?

Make careful notes of your group's views, and then discuss your findings and suggestions with other groups.

Writing

One of the points in the In the home section suggests that the information in this leaflet should be given to children 'before the teenage years'.
You are going to design a leaflet which parents might even leave lying around the house for a child of 10–11 to pick up and read.

Preparation
Bearing in mind the target audience, decide on the following and make notes:

- how much information is needed
- what information is needed
- how the information will be presented (vocabulary and 'tone', colour/black and white, photographs/illustrations/cartoons)
- how you will first attract your potential reader (title, style of print, shape of leaflet).

Overview

Write a few sentences in response to each of these questions. Wherever possible support your answer by referring to particular parts of the text.

1 How do you feel about the idea of such a leaflet for parents? How much practical use is it likely to be?

2 This leaflet is produced by The Portman Group which represents 'the drinks industry'. Does this surprise you? Why might it be to the advantage of breweries, and others, to be responsible for such an initiative?

3 The laws regarding alcohol and young people are complicated. Some say that they need updating. Are you clear what the laws are? Of which law/s do you approve? What alterations do you suggest?

4 There is pressure at the present time to turn all public houses into places where the whole family is welcomed. However there is resistance to this idea from some quarters. What arguments might each side put forward in support of its case? What is your view?

Drafting
Work with a partner for part of this section.

1 Now write a first draft of the text of the leaflet, including a list of any photographs or other illustrations you want to use.

2 Swap drafts with a partner and discuss your work and ways in which each text can be improved.

3 Now write a second draft, including the changes you have discussed.

B6 Send-offs

See: ● A11 Making notes (p34)
● A26 Comparisons (p86)

The patriot
An old story

It was roses, roses all the way,
With myrtle mixed in my path like mad:
The house-roofs seemed to heave and sway,
The church-spires flamed, such flags they had,
5   A year ago on this very day.

The air broke into a mist with bells,
The old walls rocked with the crowd and cries,
Had I said, 'Good folk, mere noise repels —
But give me your sun from yonder skies!'
10   They had answered, 'And afterward, what else?'

Alack, it was I who leaped at the sun
To give it my loving friends to keep!
Nought man could do, have I left undone:
And you see my harvest, what I reap
15   This very day, now a year is run.

There's nobody on the house-tops now —
Just a palsied few at the windows set;
For the best of the sight is, all allow,
At the Shambles' Gate — or, better yet,
20   By the very scaffold's foot, I trow.

I go in the rain, and, more than needs,
A rope cuts both my wrists behind;
And I think, by the feel, my forehead bleeds
For they fling, whoever has a mind,
25   Stones at me for my year's misdeeds.

Thus I entered, and thus I go!
In triumphs, people have dropped down dead
'Paid by the world, what dost thou owe
Me?' — God might question; now instead
30   'Tis God shall repay: I am safer so.

Robert Browning

myrtle: an evergreen shrub with sweet-smelling flowers, used as an emblem of love
palsied: shaking, trembling
Shambles: the place where animals are slaughtered or butchered
trow: believe

The send-off

Down the close, darkening lanes they sang their way
To the siding-shed,
And lined the train with faces grimly gay.
Their breasts were stuck all white with wreath and spray
5 As men's are, dead.

Dull porters watched them, and a casual tramp
Stood staring hard,
Sorry to miss them from the upland camp.
Then, unmoved, signals nodded, and a lamp
10 Winked to the guard.

So secretly, like wrongs hushed-up, they went.
They were not ours:
We never heard to which front these were sent.
Nor there if they yet mock what women meant
15 Who gave them flowers.

Shall they return to beatings of great bells
In wild train-loads?
A few, a few, too few for drums and yells,
May creep back, silent, to village wells
20 Up half-known roads.

Wilfred Owen

Preparation

Step one

Read the poems to get a feel for what they are saying as a whole.
Think about the points below.

The patriot

1 What is the speaker remembering at the beginning of the poem?
2 How long ago did it happen?
3 What had been his reaction to the way people greeted him then?
4 In what ways is the situation different now?
5 Why: what has changed?
6 What is going to happen to him?
7 What is the poem saying about patriotism, glory and war?

The send-off

1 Who are 'they'?
2 Where are they going?
3 Where have they come from?
4 Why have they gone 'secretly'?
5 What does the poet think about how they may come back?

Step two

Look at each poem and make notes about:

1 the way words are used
2 the images created
3 the feelings aroused
4 the overall picture created by the poem.

Think specifically about the points below amongst others.

The patriot

■ how the sense of wild popularity is conveyed
■ the feelings of the patriot now (look at stanzas 3 and 6)
■ the details that show how completely the crowd has turned
■ how he feels about facing God
■ what the poem gains/loses by the narrator also being the main character.

The send-off

■ the send-off that might be expected for those defending their country
■ how these particular soldiers actually went to war
  – the description of the lane
  – the description of the soldiers
  – the presence of the porters and the tramp
  – the signals and the lamp
■ the use of the question in the final stanza
■ the way the soldiers return
■ the phrase 'half-known'
■ the gains/losses by the narrator of the poem being an observer rather than a participant (the poet was himself a soldier so could easily have framed the poem differently).

Step three

What is special/distinctive about each of the two poems?
Write two or three sentences about each poem.

Some points you could consider are:

The patriot
- the contrast of then and now
- the loyalty of the crowd
- the irony in what has happened.

The send-off
- the way the poem suggests the public attitude to war
- guilt and responsibility
- the inevitability of death for many.

Step four

What are the main differences/similarities between the poems?

Think about:

1 the contrasts between the beginning and the end
2 the use of detail (especially by Owen)
3 the sense of things being beyond control
4 the sense of glamour in patriotism
5 the narrative position taken up by the writer.

Practice

Extended response to reading: critical evaluation

Sometimes a poem can make a lasting impression on us because of its subject and/or the way it is written. Choose either *The Patriot* or *The send-off*, and write a critical evaluation of the poem in which you discuss **why** the poem made an impression on you and **how** the poet achieves this.
The following structure may be useful:

1 introduce your response by saying briefly what the poem is about and why it made a lasting impression on you
2 develop your response by identifying detail in each stanza that, in your opinion, is particularly effective
3 analyse how these specific aspects of the writer's craft, for example, the use of language, including figures of speech, and other features such as rhyme and rhythm, are used within the poem
4 evaluate the overall effect of the form and content of the poem and include in your summing up why it made a lasting impression on you.

B7 The Temptation

See: **A20** Character (p62) ● **A21** Action (p66) ● **A5** Reading 'between the lines' (p17)

Nineteenth-century fiction set in Scotland often concerned itself with the unfamiliar, describing the people and the way of life in the Highlands and Islands in a manner that made them seem romantic or strange. Encounters between city dwellers and rural inhabitants were often used by authors to create mystery, as in the opening of the long story, *The Penance of John Logan*, by the Scottish author, William Black. This is from the opening chapter, called 'The Temptation'. The language is not particularly difficult, but long sentences can make it seem complicated. It is easier to follow if you pause slightly at the commas.

The summer sea was shining fair and calm, a perfect mirror of the almost cloudless heavens overhead, as a small rowing-boat, occupied by a single person, was slowly approaching a lonely little island in the Outer Hebrides. The solitary rower was neither fisherman nor sailor, but merely a holiday-maker – a well-known banker from London, in fact – who was seeking rest and recreation on the West Highlands, and who had rather a fancy for going about all by himself and for exploring out-of-the-way neighbourhoods. He had heard a good deal of this *Eilean-na-Keal* – The Island of the Burying-place – of its sculptured tombstones, its ancient chapel, its Saints' Well, and other relics and traces of the time when the early Christians made their first settlements in these sea-solitudes; and on this pleasant morning, the water being like a sheet of glass, he thought that he could not do better than hire a boat at the little village on the mainland where he chanced to be staying, and pull himself across. It is true that the nearer he got to the island, he found that there was a heavy tide running, and his labour at the oars was a much more arduous task than he had bargained for; but eventually he managed to fight his way through, the boat at last shooting into a small and sheltered bay, well out of the current.

But when he stood up to reconnoitre the shore and select a landing-place, he found to his intense astonishment that the island was not so totally uninhabited as he had been informed it was. A pair of eyes were calmly regarding him; and those eyes belonged to a little old man who was seated on a rock some way along the beach – a little, bent, broad-shouldered old man, with long white hair and tanned and weather-worn face. A further glance showed him a cumbrous and dilapidated rowing-boat hauled up into a kind of creek, and also a number of lobster-traps lying about on the shingle. The new-comer therefore naturally concluded that he had not been forestalled by any such hateful being as a fellow-tourist, but merely by an old lobster-fisherman who had come out to look after his traps.

The Englishman shoved his boat through the seaweed, jumped out, and hauled it up on the beach; and then walked along to the little old man, who had ceased mending his lobster-traps, and was still calmly regarding the stranger.

'Good morning!' the latter said, cheerfully – he was a good-humoured-looking, middle-aged person, who had knocked about the world sufficiently, and who liked to converse with whomsoever he chanced to meet. 'This is rather a lonely place for you to be in, isn't it?'

'Ay,' said the old man, as he carefully scrutinised the other from head to heel, 'there's not many comes here.'

'But there used to be people living on the island?' Mr. Ramsden continued, chiefly for the sake of getting his new acquaintance to talk.

The old man paused for a moment or two; then he slowly made answer –

'Ay, I have heard that.'

Was he half-witted, then, or was his English defective, or was it his lonely life that had made him thus chary and hesitating of speech? He seemed to ponder over the questions, his eyes all the while taking note of every detail of the stranger's features and dress.

'I saw some seals as I came along: are there many of them about here?'

'Ay, plenty.'

'Don't people come and shoot them?'

'No.'

'Doesn't anybody ever come here?'

chary: cautious

'No.'

50 'Do you ever have to pass the night here?'

'Ay.'

'Where do you sleep, then – in your boat?'

He shook his head.

'Where then?'

55 'In the chapel.'

'Oh, that's the chapel I've heard about: you must come and show me where it is, if you are not too busy. Have you been getting many lobsters lately?'

'Some.'

'What do you do with them? You can't have many customers in Harivaig.'

60 'To London,' the old man said, laconically.

'Oh, you send them to London? To a fishmonger, or a fish-dealer, perhaps?'

'Ay, do ye know him?' And then old John Logan seemed to wake up a little; indeed, he spoke almost eagerly, though he was continually hesitating for want of the proper word. 'Do ye know him? – Corstorphine – Billingsgate – he sends

65 me the boxes. Do ye know him? – bekass – bekass he is not giffing me enough – and if there wass another one now I would go aweh from him. Mebbe you know Corstorphine?'

'No; I'm sorry to say I don't. I should be very glad to help you if I could, but I'm afraid you would run a great risk in giving up a constant customer. I suppose

70 he takes whatever you send?'

'Oh, ay; oh ay,' was the old man's answer, 'but he does not gif enough! And – and I hef a young lass at home – she is the daughter of my daughter that's dead – and – and she is going to be married; and the young man – he is for buying a – a part in a herring-smack, and I am for helping him with the money. But

75 Corstorphine should gif more.'

William Black: *The Penance of John Logan*

Standard Grade English – Credit

Preparation

First thoughts

What questions does the extract raise on a first reading about:

■ the banker, Mr Ramsden?
■ the lobster-fisherman, John Logan?
■ the island?

Make a note of your questions.
Check at the end of your work to see how many are solved and how many remain unanswered.

Closer reading

Look at the following statements.
Decide whether they are true or false.
Find evidence from the passage for each of your answers.

1 The banker does not enjoy the company of other people.
2 The lobster-fisherman cannot understand what Mr Ramsden says to him.
3 The lobster-fisherman is in need of money.
4 The banker thinks that the lobster-fisherman is foolish.
5 The island is a peaceful place.

Character and relationship

1 What do we learn about the banker from this extract? Go through the text again, collecting all the information you can find. Set it out in a table with these headings:

- What he looks like
- What he does and how he does it
- How he speaks
- What he thinks
- Other information.

2 Look at the information you have collected. What else can you work out about the banker based on these details? Write any other notes below the table.
3 Now do the same for the lobster-fisherman.
4 Think about the relationship that is emerging between the two characters. Look for information about how they:

- behave towards each other
- speak to each other.

Make notes on the conclusions you come to.

Setting

5 Describe briefly where and when this scene takes place. For each statement you make give the number(s) of the line(s) where this information is to be found.
6 How would you describe the atmosphere of this scene?

Look at the list of words below and choose any that you think are suitable to describe the atmosphere. Add any others that you can think of.

sinister	exciting	unusual
bright	gloomy	tranquil
sombre	peculiar	menacing
amusing	mysterious	tense
forbidding	entertaining	odd

Plot

The two characters are on the island for quite different reasons and, in talking, they reveal things about themselves.

7 In the opening section, we learn about the banker's reason for being on the island. What does he hope to find there? How does he react when he finds he is not alone?
8 When the lobster-fisherman speaks, we learn about the problems he faces. What are these? How does he link the banker with his problems?
9 What do you think might happen on the island?

Writing about the text

10 Imagine that you are directing a film version of this scene. Think about the atmosphere you want to convey. (Look back at your responses to questions 5 and 6.) Make a list of the shots or images you could use to do this. Write a description of the beginning of the film as it appears to the viewer. Describe it in detail, shot by shot, up to the point where the dialogue begins.
11 Write a description of the character and appearance of the banker and of the lobster-fisherman. Make sure that you support what you say by referring to the text.

Writing a story

Write your own short story in which two people from different backgrounds meet in an out-of-the-way place. Think about:

1 your two main characters:

- what they look like
- how they behave

2 the setting in which the encounter takes place

3 how to keep your readers wondering what is going to happen.

B8 image breakers

See:
- **A6** Fact and opinion (p20)
- **A8** Purposes for writing (p26)
- **A10** Tone and formality (p32)
- **A16** Argument and persuasion (p49)
- **A26** Comparisons (p86)

When an advertising agency was given the job of re-launching Skoda, they had a massive problem: the cars had been the subject of jokes for as long as anyone could remember.
For example:

Question: *What do you call a sewing machine on wheels?*
Answer: *A Skoda.*

1 What cars can you think of that have an image problem in the same way as Skoda had?
2 Why do some cars have an image problem?
3 What other things can you think of that have an image problem?

Think particularly about clothes, music and shops but cover any other areas that you wish.

The Spastics Society went even further to change their image. Because so many people associated the word 'spastic' with an inability to do things, they decided to change the name of the charity to Scope. There is a little less information in their advertisement but the intention is the same: to change attitudes.

Cerebral palsy is the medical name for this condition which results from damage to an unborn baby's developing brain. The part affected is that section of the brain which controls the way that our bodies move. The damage can sometimes affect mental ability, but not in all cases. There are many very bright people with cerebral palsy.

4 What other disabilities get treated with a lack of understanding? Why?
5 Why do people tend to link disability with lack of intelligence?

Look at the advertisements on the following pages before answering the questions on page 125.

Standard Grade English – Credit

121

Before we changed the car, we changed the company.

A car can tell you a lot about the company that made it.

When a company changes, the changes are visible in the cars that they make. At Skoda, over the past four years, we have changed more than any car maker in the world.

We've had to look long and hard at what we've been getting right, and what we've been getting wrong.

The good news.

People who buy our cars, like our cars. We've been getting the basics right. Price. Reliability. Engineering. And in Europe's leading customer satisfaction audit, J.D. Power*, Skoda beats the likes of BMW, Rover and Ford.

People who knew about cars, knew our history. For the first half of the century we were one of the world's greatest marques. When we built Hispano-Suizas, they were the most elegant cars on the road. When the cold war started, that all stopped. And the years of isolation took their toll.

The other news.

What we were getting wrong was, basically, everything else.

Volkswagen Group

We were too "inward-looking". We made the cars we wanted to make, rather than the cars most customers wanted. So, our cars have never had a "fashionable" image.

Conclusion: we had good people, but were using them in the wrong way. It had to change. It wasn't easy. It never is.

The change.

Volkswagen invested a huge amount of cash and expertise. We revolutionised our quality control systems. Totally revised our design processes. Everything was scrutinised by Volkswagen, everything.

We turned the company around.

The evidence.

You can see these changes in our new car, the Felicia. It's not what you'd expect from a Skoda.

It doesn't look the way you'd expect a Skoda to look. It doesn't feel the way you'd expect a Skoda to feel.

But it still gives you what Skoda always did: more car for less money.

We heard the criticisms. We changed our company. We changed our cars. Now, are you open enough to change your mind?

We've changed the car. Can you change your mind?

For a full information pack about the new Felicia, call 0345 745745. We'll also tell you where to find your nearest Skoda dealer.

*April 1995.

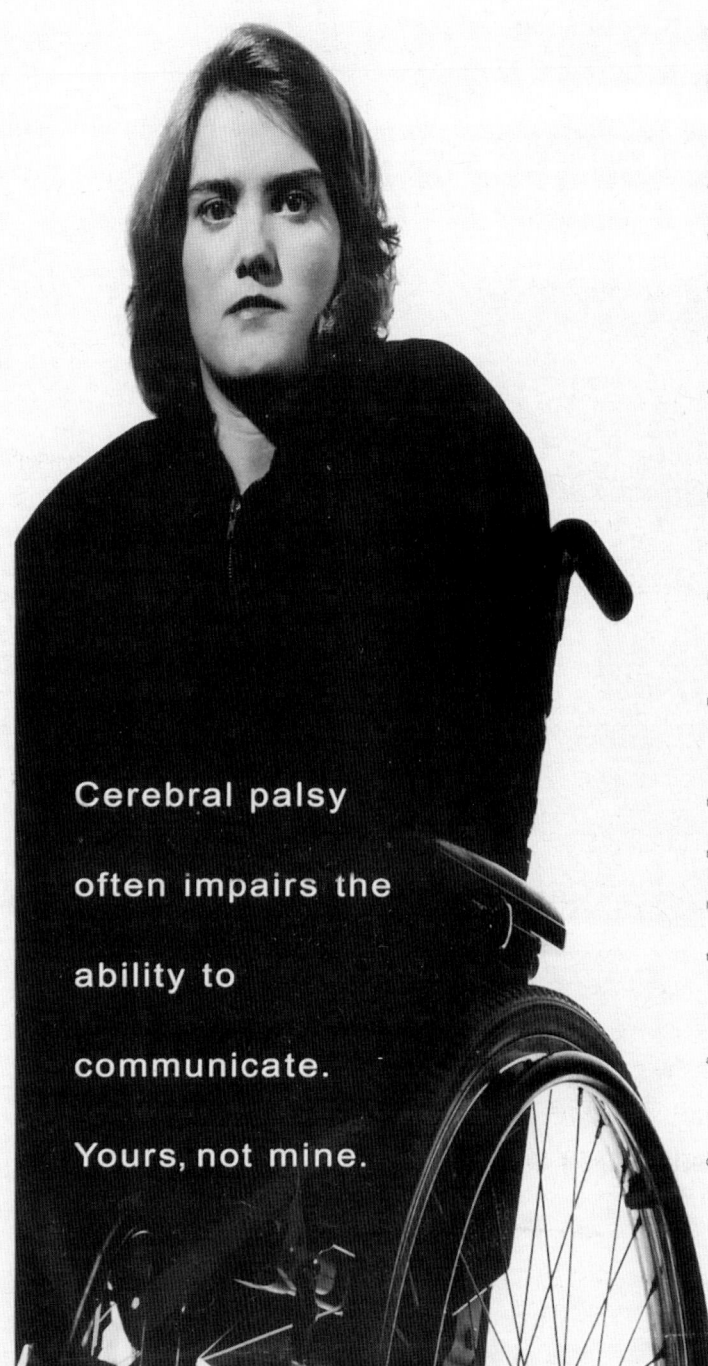

Cerebral palsy
often impairs the
ability to
communicate.
Yours, not mine.

I know it's difficult to understand what

I say. But it would be easier if people tried.

It's the muscles in my jaw and my

tongue that are affected, not my mind. That

works as clearly as you're reading this.

And I don't care how many times you

ask me to repeat myself. I'd rather you do

that than just nod and pretend you under-

stand. For all you know, I might have just

told you that you've got a face like a bull-

dog sucking a wasp. Not that I would.

The worst thing is when people just

ignore me and look the other way.

Schools, employers, local authorities,

I've been ignored by them all.

And like everyone else with cerebral

palsy, I'm tired of it.

So are the Spastics Society. That's why

they changed to Scope. Because it's about

time that everyone with cerebral palsy,

however severely disabled, was allowed

the scope to live normally.

Which means not having our rights and

abilities ignored.

Scope are as keen to talk to you as I am.

Call them, local rate, on 0645 486 487.

SCOPE
FOR PEOPLE WITH CEREBRAL PALSY

Formerly The Spastics Society

Practice

What the advertisements are trying to do

Answer these questions in your own words as far as possible.

Skoda

1 Look at the first three paragraphs of the advertisement.

   - What do Skoda say they have been doing?
   - What claim is made about the changes taking place?

2 Look at the section headed 'The good news'.

   - In their view, what has been working well?
   - In what ways does the section try to impress the reader?

3 Look at the section headed 'The other news'.

   - What was the company's main fault?
   - Why is this section not called 'The bad news'?

4 Look at the section called 'The change'.

   - Choose the words and phrases that you think give an impression of great change and explain why you have chosen them.

5 Look at the section headed 'The evidence'.

   - How is this section appealing to a potential buyer?

6 Look at the advertisement as a whole including the photographs.

   - What are the main selling points?
   - What is your view of the success of the advertisement? Give reasons for your view.

Scope

7 What misunderstanding is addressed in the first two paragraphs of this advertisement?

8 The third paragraph deals with a particular problem. Explain what the problem is and how it can be overcome.

9 What is the importance of the change in the name of the charity?

10 How would you describe the tone of the advertisement? Why do you think this tone is used?

Practice

Writing

How successfully can an advertisement change people's attitudes?
Look back at the two advertisements you have studied, and write about:

- how these two advertisements capture your attention
- the ways in which they seek to convince you
- their overall effect on you.

Use ideas from the ten answers in the Preparation section but do not simply string those answers together. A useful possible structure would be:

- two opening paragraphs, one looking at each advertisement
- a number of paragraphs looking at the detail of the first advertisement
- a number of paragraphs looking at the detail of the second advertisement
- a closing paragraph summing up the overall effects and comparing them.

New schools for old

Every time there is a special event for parents, most teachers have the same complaint: 'We never see the parents we really wanted to see.' The reason for this is that there are plenty of parents who do not enjoy going into schools if they can avoid it. Their own schooldays have put them off for life. When you hear some of the stories of what used to go on in school, you can hardly blame them (assuming you believe the stories that parents tell).

Your school wants to run an open day or evening that is especially directed at parents who do not normally come into school unless they are forced to.

Assignment

Your task is to create an informative piece of advertising that makes such parents feel that schools might be very different places today from what they were like 20 or 30 years ago.

To do this, you will need to do some research by talking to your parents and people of your parents' age. Here are five basic questions that you can use as a starting point:

1 What subjects did you study in school?
2 What were the teachers like?
3 What was discipline like?
4 What activities took place in a lesson?
5 How did pupils behave towards each other?

Preparing your publicity

As you work on this publicity for parents, think about these things:

■ How are you going to present it?
■ What are your main points?
■ What headings/sub-headings will you use?
■ What artwork would you like?
■ Which places in your school might you photograph?

B9 Love, Death and Betrayal

See:
- **A25** Rhyme and rhythm (p82)
- **A26** Comparisons (p86)

A popular poetic form, dating back to the Middle Ages, is the ballad. This unit contains two ballads, one several centuries old and one from the twentieth century.

The unquiet grave

'The wind doth blow today, my love,
And a few small drops of rain;
I never had but one true love;
In cold grave she was lain.

5 I'll do as much for my true love
As any young man may;
I'll sit and mourn all at her grave
For a twelvemonth and a day.'

The twelvemonth and a day being up,
10 The dead began to speak:
'Oh who sits weeping on my grave
And will not let me sleep?'

''Tis I, my love, sits on your grave,
And will not let you sleep;
15 For I crave one kiss of your clay-cold lips
And that is all I seek.'

'You crave one kiss of my clay-cold lips;
But my breath smells earthy strong;
If you have one kiss of my clay-cold lips
20 Your time will not be long.

'Tis down in yonder garden green,
Love, where we used to walk,
The finest flower that ere was seen
Is withered to a stalk.

25 The stalk is withered dry, my love,
So will our hearts decay;
So make yourself content, my love,
Till death calls you away.'

Anonymous

Standard Grade English – Credit

Preparation

First thoughts

Write brief answers to these questions. For each answer make sure that you can quote from the text to support what you say.

1 Who is speaking at the beginning of the poem ('Speaker A')?
2 To whom is A speaking?
3 What is the mood of the opening of the poem?
4 What do you think is the background story to the poem?
5 Who speaks in the third verse ('Speaker B')?
6 Is there anything to prove that A and B are:
   ■ young or old?
   ■ male or female?
   How do you imagine them?
7 What does A want from B?
8 What is B's response?

True or false

Look at these statements about *The unquiet grave*. For each one:

■ state whether you think it is true or false
■ explain your reasons
■ if a statement is false or misleading, try to produce an accurate one to replace it.

1 The poem is about the love of a young man and a young woman.
2 The young man in the poem is a loyal and faithful lover.
3 The woman who was his love is heartless.
4 The withered flower represents their love which has died.
5 The poem is about coming to terms with tragedy.
6 The poem is telling us that all love is doomed.

Looking at the form

For each answer in this section, make sure that you can quote from the text to support what you say.

1 What is the rhyme scheme of the poem?
2 What is the basic metre?
3 In the Middle Ages ballads were performed to a musical accompaniment. Is there anything in the form of this poem that suggests this?
4 The performer had to know his material by heart. Are there any features of this poem that would make that easier?

Looking at the language

1 Look through the poem for words and images referring to weather. Write them down.
2 Now do the same for words and images referring to:
   ■ warmth/cold
   ■ moisture/dryness
   ■ living things/dying things
3 The words and images you have collected play an important part in determining the overall impact of the poem. How would you describe their effect?

Ballad

O! shairly ye hae seen my love
Doun whaur the waters wind:
He walks like ane wha fears nae man
And yet his e'en are kind.

O! shairly ye hae seen my love   5
At the turnin o' the tide;
For then he gethers in the nets
Doun be the waterside.

O! lassie I hae seen your love
At the turnin o' the tide;   10
And he was wi' the fisher-folk
Doun be the waterside.

The fisher-folk were at their trade
No far frae Walnut Grove;
They gether'd in their dreepin nets   15
And fund your ain true love.

William Soutar

Preparation

First thoughts

Write brief answers to these questions. For each answer make sure that you can quote from the text to support what you say.

1 What is the background situation to the poem?
2 When do you think it might be set?
3 All of the verses of the poem, except for the last, follow the same pattern. What is it?
4 Are there any clues to suggest who the speakers are?
5 What ideas have you formed about the speakers' previous histories?

True or false

Look at these statements about *Ballad*. For each one:

■ state whether you think it is true or false
■ explain your reasons
■ if a statement is false or misleading, try to produce an accurate one to replace it.

1 The poem is about a man and a woman who are lovers.
2 One of the two speakers is a fisherman.
3 The poem suggests that all love is doomed.
4 The drowned man died in an accident.

Looking at form and language

For each answer in this section, make sure that you can quote from the text to support what you say.

1 What is the rhyme scheme of the poem?
2 What is the basic metre?
3 What use does the poem make of repetition?
4 Ballads often tell their story by picking out physical details and letting them do the work (like the withered flower in *The unquiet grave*). Does this ballad follow a similar approach?
5 How does the sense of threat increase as the poem develops?

Analysis: What is a ballad like?

Some of the main features of ballads are these:

1 regular rhyme pattern
2 regular rhythm
3 pattern of repetition, often in the form of a chorus
4 common subjects – love, death, betrayal, bravery
5 lack of detailed description
6 use of dialogue
7 supernatural happenings
8 parts of the story left unexplained
9 characters/situations are often stereotypical.

Not all ballads have all these features but they are found in many of them.
Which of these features is shown by each of the ballads you have been reading?

Practice

Coursework

Writing

1 Write a comparison of *The unquiet grave* and *Ballad*, in which you show
   similarities and differences of subject matter, language and form.
2 How do the ballads you have been studying compare with other forms of storytelling
   in verse? Compare the storytelling in the two ballads with two other poems that tell a
   story. Either make your own choice of poems, or compare these two ballads with
   The patriot on page 113 and *The send-off* on page 114.

   ■ What qualities does each poem have?
   ■ Which poem or poems do you prefer and why?
   ■ What different effects are achieved by the different forms?

Coursework

Visualising the poem

If you were preparing to make a video to
promote *Ballad* by William Soutar, what shots
would you plan? Prepare a scenario for four
scenes you would like to shoot. One example is
provided opposite.

When you have completed your scenario, write
an explanation for the director of how you think
the film you have planned will bring the poem
to life.

Scene 1: Scenario

Aerial view of village street.
People are busy on the street, some carrying
baskets, some mending nets.
Shot identifies and closes in on a young and
handsome man walking along the street.
Close-up of his face. He nods, smiles to
people he passes.

B10 An interview with

Jeremy Irons

See: ● **A5** Reading 'between the lines' (p17)
● **A6** Fact and opinion (p20)
● **A16** Argument and persuasion (p49)

The feature interview is a popular item in newspapers and magazines. Some newspapers employ a 'star' journalist who has a national reputation for such interviews. Here Lynn Barber interviews a famous film actor. At different stages there are some questions to guide your thinking.

This is not an objective article. I don't want to give a cool appraisal of Jeremy Irons, or even to be snide. I just want to boil him in oil.

A month ago I had no strong views on Jeremy Irons. He was a tall, handsome English actor who was good in *Brideshead*. Then a nice PR asked if I'd like to see a preview of *Danny, the Champion of the World*, starring Jeremy and his ten-year-old son Sam Irons, with a view to interviewing him. I saw the film, I liked it, I said yes.

My diary thereafter has scratched-out appointments with Jeremy Irons on practically every day. I was supposed to meet him in the Groucho Club, at home, in a photographer's studio. One day I was supposed to have lunch with him but he cancelled at a few hours' notice because he 'didn't like to eat and talk at the same time'. The PR was often almost sobbing as he delivered these messages to me.

This continued for three weeks or more. Finally there came a morning when I had a 10.30 a.m. appointment with Jeremy Irons at a West End hotel and the PR didn't phone to cancel. I assumed that this was a mere oversight, but went along anyway.

I sat and waited. At 10.50 Jeremy Irons sauntered in. He didn't apologize for his lateness, he didn't say hello or shake hands, he said: 'Well, we all know who we are and why we're here – let's get on with it.'

Jeremy Irons threw himself back on a sofa and lit the first of many cigarettes, not offering me one. 'Well?' he said. I started to ask him a question, but in the middle he suddenly got to his feet, walked over to the window and started fiddling with the curtains. 'I hate things to be done wrong,' he announced. 'For instance, this tieback' – and he took the curtain tieback off its hook and turned it over – 'was designed a certain way and somebody went to all the trouble of making it that certain way. So it would be quite nice to have it hang- ing the right way up. There!' And he put the tieback back on its hook and resumed his seat.

A waiter comes in with coffee and, in pouring the coffee, he spills some. Jeremy Irons points this out. He watches, eyes glittering, fin- gers drumming, while the waiter mops it up. The waiter, who had entered the room a confident and happy man, slinks away, broken.

Is Jeremy Irons, I wonder aloud, the sort of person who would watch someone doing the washing-up and then tell them they were doing it badly? 'Yes,' he agrees. 'I'm impossible. Intolerant, impatient and impossible. I'm *appalled* by sloppy work and if I see something done badly – props, for example – I say so. It's what I call profes- sionalism.'

Professionalism, bah! How often I have heard actors trotting out that tired excuse for their own behaviour. What professionalism actu- ally means is doing one's own job well: it does not include telling other people how to do theirs.

I wouldn't like to be a *tea boy* on a Jeremy Irons film, let alone a fellow actor.

First impressions

1 What are your first impressions of Jeremy Irons from reading this?

2 Why do you think he was so difficult to pin down? Is it possible to defend his behaviour?

3 What impressions do you get of the interviewer, Lynn Barber?

4 Some people dislike this approach to interviewing. They argue that the interviewer's job is just to find out about their subject's life and work and then present it to the reader. The reader does not want to know about the interviewer's thoughts and feelings. Would you agree?

What on earth must it have been like for his son working with him? Sam, to be fair, seems perfectly happy in the film, a natural actor with limitless, unforced charm; it is Jeremy Irons as his father who seems awkwardly miscast.

Why did he make *Danny, the Champion of the World*? He admit- ted that as an acting role it was not exciting and he 'played it like a £30-a-day actor' but he'd been 'acting his socks off' in *Dead Ringers* so he didn't mind.

The appeal of *Danny*, he explained, was that he could do it with his family (Sam, and also his father-in-law, Cyril Cusack, the Irish actor) just ten minutes from his home in Oxfordshire. And also it was a great vehicle for Sam …

But wasn't it rather dangerous, I suggested, putting a child into the hothouse atmosphere of film-making? Mightn't it turn his head, and make it hard for him to settle back at school? Jeremy Irons sighed: 'You're sounding very much like my wife' (the actress Sinead Cusack). 'She was very unsure about it. She is much less sanguine than I am. She argued and argued about it, saying it was dangerous.' So why override her objections?

sanguine: optimistic

'Because it's a *wonderful* experience for a child to go to work with a parent. It means they're part of the parent's *life*. So that was the positive side, and the fact that I was there to keep a close eye on him. When he finished, two things he said stick in my mind. Someone said to him, "I expect you want to be an actor?" and he said, "No. But I'd quite like to be a lighting cameraman." And then I asked him a few weeks later, "Do you miss it – the filming?" and he said "Yes I do. I miss the attention." And I thought, Well that's quite good because, of course, that's the main thing you get – attention – and he sees it very clearly.'

Jeremy Irons realized at the beginning of his career, when he did *Brideshead* and *The French Lieutenant's Woman*, that he was in danger of becoming 'Hollywood's resident Englishman', so he went off to do a Polish film, *Moonlighting*, and seasons at Stratford and on Broadway.

He believes in chasing hard after parts he wants. He wrote to the producer of *Brideshead* offering himself for Charles Ryder, and he moved heaven and earth to try to get the Robert Redford part in *Out of Africa*.

'I rang Meryl, I wrote to the producer, I worked really hard for that part. I knew that Redford was bored with acting and that he was absolutely wrong for the role – too old and American – but Redford was a friend of the producer and that was how the deal was set up.'

Positives?

5 What picture do you get of Jeremy Irons as a father?
6 What impression do you get of him as a career actor?
7 Do these aspects of him help to present a more positive image?

He turned forty last September but sighs irritably at mention of his age. 'I don't feel forty. I *feel* twenty-eight and always will. But I think the forties are a wonderful decade for a man. I see them very separately from my thirties. When I was thirty I made a big career

decision. I told the company that was trying to screw me over, to stop
95   me making *French Lieutenant's Woman*, to get lost, and I won that
battle. So at thirty I thought, "Right, you're your own man." And I
went through my thirties with great vigour and pushed hard for my
career. Now maybe that youthful arrogance is settling a bit ...'

I told him he was still 'very good-looking' and he beamed. He
100   adores compliments. If you mention that you liked his performance
in so and so, he says, 'Oh, how exactly? Tell me more.' It is a trait all
actors share but I have rarely encountered it in such an insatiable
form. But to get back to his looks ...

'I've never thought of myself as good-looking, which I think is
105   useful. If I'm shot at the right angle and with the right lens, I can look
all right. And yes, I know the angle and the lens. You see,' he says
turning his right profile towards me, 'you don't want to look at this
too often. It's all right in three-quarters, but not full profile. My right
cheek is hollower here' – tracing a line down his strangely flat cheek
110   – 'the bone is higher, the jaw not so square. It's just not such a good
profile.'

Did he tell directors that, or leave them to work it out for themselves? 'I tell them. The left profile is the one to use if you want me to
look creamy. The other profile looks more vulnerable.'

115   When he has to bare his body for a part, he spends weeks in the
gym beforehand, pumping iron. 'It's really my back muscles that I
have to work on: I have very strong arms and legs. I hate going to the
gym but it's necessary sometimes.'

Would he mind the advent of grey hairs? 'No. I actually found the
120   first one the other day. I was *rather* pleased. Enough people have said
to me, "You're going to be *wonderful* as you get older," for me not to
worry about it.' One of the odd things about him is that, although he
has the right looks and the right sort of ruthlessness, he has never
been a great ladykiller. He married his first wife when he was just
125   twenty-one, at Bristol Old Vic. That was 'a total disaster' and lasted a
year, but he soon fell for Sinead Cusack – and went to considerable
pains to get his first marriage annulled, so that they could marry in a
Catholic church. The marriage went through 'a sticky patch' in the
early eighties, but now seems steady.

130   Jeremy agreed that he could have been a Lothario but wasn't: 'It's
terribly tiring, I imagine. And I've never needed to do that. I mean,
the logic seems to me that if you find someone you love, you want to
stay with them, and that means marriage. Also, I believe you have to
make a commitment to get joy. It's the old Puritan ethic: you have to
135   put something in to get something out.'

He also values security. When he was fifteen his father made him
take a vocational guidance test. One of the options was the theatre
but the report said: 'Not right for you because you need too much
security.'

140   'But I think it's the security that my family gives me that enables
me to take risks in my profession,' he explains. 'The analogy is with a

trait: feature
insatiable: incapable
of being satisfied

Lothario: ladykiller

Puritan ethic: the
belief that the only
good thing is to work
hard and that you can
never gain anything
worthwhile without
hard work
analogy: comparison,
parallel

castle, and I ride out on my white charger, but I know I can always come back to the castle.'

Like most people, probably, I first saw Jeremy Irons in *Brideshead Revisited* and formed my image of him on the basis of that role. This was to underestimate his considerable powers as an actor. He is intelligent and articulate, like Charles Ryder, but he is not, like him, wet and ineffectual. On the contrary, he seems ruthless, arrogant and generally contemptuous of other people. He can still, he claims, 'turn on the creamy Brideshead charm' when he wants to, but nowadays he seldom bothers. At no point in our conversation did he say anything kind or generous about anyone else.

And at the end, when he still hadn't mentioned, let alone apologized for, our two dozen cancelled appointments, I raised the subject myself. 'Oh that,' he said airily. 'It was the publicity people's fault. They just can't do their jobs.'

articulate: able to express himself clearly and fully

Lynn Barber: *Mostly Men*

Preparation

Fact or opinion?

Clearly Lynn Barber includes a lot of her own (strongly held) opinions in this article. She also provides us with a lot of factual information about Jeremy Irons' life and work.

1 Make a list of all the facts you can find in the article
2 Use them to make an entry in a biographical reference book, like the one shown below.
   You should aim to make this as detailed as possible.

OLIVIER, Laurence, English actor, director and man of the theatre. Known for his performance of all the great Shakespearian roles on the stage, including

Preparation

Speaking positively

While an initial impression may be that Lynn Barber paints a very negative picture of her subject, we also learn many positive things about him. In addition some of his apparently negative features could be presented in a positive way.

1 Make a list of all the positive things you can find in the article about the actor – with evidence where possible.

Practice

Coursework

2 Use your notes to write up a 'Star Profile' for a popular magazine.

Practice

Coursework

Jeremy's diary

We learn a lot in the article about Jeremy Irons' life and opinions. Suppose he writes a detailed diary each day, describing what has happened and the people he has met, and expressing his thoughts and feelings about them. How would he have written about:

■ the day of the interview?
■ the day the article is published and he reads it?

Write those two diary entries.

Rumours about you

B11

See: ● **A20** Character (p62)
● **A21** Action (p66)
● **A5** Reading 'between the lines' (p17)

This unit contains these elements:

■ a complete short story
■ at regular intervals, questions to guide your reading. You can use these as you read, or while you read the story for a second time. You may find it useful to write short note-form answers
■ at the end a variety of shorter and longer activities to broaden and deepen your response to the story.

'Sit down, young man,' said the Official.

'Thanks.' The young man sat.

'I've been hearing rumours about you,' the Official said pleasantly. 'Oh, nothing much. Your nervousness. Your not
5   getting on so well. Several months now I've heard about you, and I thought I'd call you in. Thought maybe you'd like your job changed. Like to go overseas, work in some other War Area? Desk job killing you off, like to get right in on the old fight?'

'I don't think so,' said the young sergeant.

10   'What *do* you want?'

The sergeant shrugged and looked at his hands. 'To live in peace. To learn that during the night, somehow, the guns of the world had rusted, the bacteria had turned sterile in their bomb
15   casings, the tanks had sunk like prehistoric monsters into roads suddenly made tar pits. That's what I'd like.'

'That's what we'd all like, of course,' said the Official. 'Now stop all that idealistic
20   chatter and tell me where you'd like to be sent. You have your choice – the Western or Northern War Zone.' The Official tapped a pink map on his desk.

But the sergeant was talking at his hands,
turning them over, looking at the fingers: 'What
would you officers do, what would we men do,
what would the *world* do if we all woke tomorrow
with the guns in flaking ruin?'

The Official saw that he would have to deal
carefully with the sergeant. He smiled quietly.
'That's an interesting question. I like to talk about
such theories, and my answer is that there'd be
mass panic. Each nation would think itself the
only unarmed nation in the world, and would
blame its enemies for the disaster. There'd be
waves of suicide, stocks collapsing, a million
tragedies.'

'But *after* that,' the sergeant said. 'After they
realised it was true, that every nation was
disarmed and there was nothing more to fear, if
we were all clean to start over fresh and new, what
then?'

'They'd rearm as swiftly as possible.'

'What if they could be stopped?'

'Then they'd beat each other with their fists. If
it got down to that. Huge armies of men with
boxing gloves of steel pikes would gather at the
national borders. And if you took the gloves away
they'd use their fingernails and feet. And if you
cut their legs off they'd *spit* on each other. And if
you cut off their tongues and stopped their
mouths with corks they'd fill the atmosphere so
full of hate that mosquitoes would drop to the
ground and birds would fall dead from telephone
wires.'

'Then you don't think it would do any good?'
the sergeant said.

'Certainly not. It'd be like ripping the carapace
off a turtle. Civilisation would gasp and die from
shock.'

carapace:
shell

The young man shook his head. 'Or are you lying to yourself and me because you've a nice comfortable job?'

'Let's call it ninety per cent cynicism, ten per cent rationalising the situation. Go put your Rust away and forget about it.'

65   The sergeant jerked his head up. 'How'd you know I *had* it?' he said. 'Had what?'

'The Rust, of course.'

'What're you talking about?'

'I *can* do it, you know. I could start the Rust tonight if I wanted to.'

70   The Official laughed. 'You can't be serious.'

'I am. I've been meaning to come talk to you. I'm glad you called me in. I've worked on this invention for a long time. It's been a dream of mine. It has to do with the structure of certain atoms. If you study them you find that the arrangement of atoms in steel armour is such-and-

75   such an arrangement. I was looking for an imbalance factor. I majored in physics and metallurgy, you know. It came to me, there's a Rust factor in the air all the time. Water vapour. I had to find a way to give steel a nervous breakdown. Then the water vapour everywhere in the world would take over. Not on all metal, of course. Our civilisation is

80   built on steel, I wouldn't want to destroy most buildings. I'd just eliminate guns and shells, tanks, planes, battleships. I can set the machine to work on copper and brass and aluminium, too, if necessary I'd just walk by all of those weapons and just being near them I'd make them fall away.'

85   The Official was bending over his desk, staring at the sergeant. 'May I ask you a question?'

'Yes.'

'Have you ever thought you were Christ?'

'I can't say that I have. But I have considered that God was good to

90   me to let me find what I was looking for, if that's what you mean.'

The Official reached into his breast pocket and drew out an expensive ball-point pen capped with a rifle shell. He flourished the pen and started filling in a form. 'I want you to take this to Dr Mathews this afternoon, for a complete check-up. Not that I expect anything

95   really bad, understand. But don't you feel you *should* see a doctor?'

'You think I'm lying about my machine,' said the sergeant. 'I'm not. It's so small it can be hidden in this cigarette package. The effect of it extends for nine hundred miles. I could tour this country in a few days, with the machine set to a certain type of steel. The other nations

100   couldn't take advantage of us because I'd rust their weapons as they approach us. Then I'd fly to Europe. By this time next month the world would be free of war forever. I don't know how I found this invention. It's impossible. Just as impossible as the atom bomb. I've waited a month now, trying to think it over. I worried about what would happen

105   if I did rip off the carapace, as you say. But now I've just decided. My talk with you has helped clarify things. Nobody thought an aeroplane would ever fly, nobody thought an atom would ever explode, and nobody thinks that there can ever be Peace, but there *will* be.'

cynicism: always looking to cast scorn on the value of things. A cynic has been described as a person who knows the price of everything and the value of nothing

metallurgy: the study of the properties of metals

Questions

1   When do you think this story is set and why?
2   What do you think the Official's job is exactly?
3   What did the sergeant do for a living?
4   What does he want to achieve?
5   What is the Official's view of war and human nature?
6   Why does he want the sergeant to see a doctor?

'Take that paper over to Dr Mathews, will you?' said the
110 Official hastily.

The sergeant got up. 'You're not going to assign me to any
new Zone then?'

'Not right away, no. I've changed my mind. We'll let Mathews
decide.'

115 'I've decided then,' said the young man. 'I'm leaving the post within
the next few minutes. I've a pass. Thank you very much for giving me
your valuable time, sir.'

'Now look here, Sergeant, don't take things so seriously. You don't
have to leave. Nobody's going to hurt you.'

120 'That's right. Because nobody would believe me. Goodbye, sir.' The
sergeant opened the office door and stepped out.

The door shut and the Official was alone. He stood for a moment
looking at the door. He sighed. He rubbed his hands over his face.
The phone rang. He answered it abstractedly.

125 'Oh, *hello*, Doctor. I was just going to call you.' A pause. 'Yes, I was
going to send him over to you. Look, is it all right for that young man
to be wandering about? It *is* all right? If you say so, Doctor. Probably
needs a rest, a good long one. Poor boy has a delusion of rather an
interesting sort. Yes, yes. It's a shame. But that's what a Sixteen-Year
130 War can do to you, I suppose.'

The phone voice buzzed in reply.

The Official listened and nodded. 'I'll make a note on that. Just a
second.' He reached for his ball-point pen. 'Hold on a moment.
Always mislaying things.' He patted his pocket. 'Had my pen here a
135 moment ago. Wait.' He put down the phone and searched his desk,
pulling out drawers. He checked his blouse pocket again. He stopped
moving. Then his hands twitched slowly into his pocket and probed
down. He poked his thumb and forefinger deep and brought out a
pinch of something.

abstractedly:
not concentrating,
with his mind on
other things

140   He sprinkled it on his desk blotter: a small filtering powder of yellow-red rust.

        He sat staring at it for a moment. Then he picked up the phone. 'Mathews,' he said, 'get off the line, quick.' There was a click of someone hanging up and then he dialled another call. 'Hello, Guard

145   Station, listen, there's a man coming past you any minute now, you know him, name of Sergeant Hollis, stop him, shoot him down, kill him if necessary, don't ask questions, kill the son of a bitch, you heard me, this is the Official talking! Yes, kill him, you hear!'

        'But sir,' said a bewildered voice on the other end of the line. 'I

150   can't, I just *can't* ...'

        'What do you mean, you can't, God damn it!'

        'Because ...' the voice faded away. You could hear the guard breathing into the phone a mile away.

        The Official shook the phone. 'Listen to me, listen, get your gun

155   ready!'

        'I can't shoot anyone,' said the guard.

        The Official sank back in his chair. He sat blinking for half a minute, gasping.

        Out there even now – he didn't have to look, no one had to tell him

160   – the hangars were dusting down in soft red rust, and the aeroplanes were blowing away on a brown-rust wind into nothingness, and the tanks were sinking, sinking slowly into the hot asphalt roads, like dinosaurs (isn't that what the man had said?) sinking into primordial tar pits. Trucks were blowing away in ochre puffs of smoke, their

165   drivers dumped by the road, with only the tyres left running on the highways.

        'Sir ...' said the guard, who was seeing all this, far away. 'Oh, God ...'

        'Listen, listen!' screamed the Official. 'Go after him, get him, with your hands, choke him, with your fists, beat him, use your feet, kick his

170   ribs in, kick him to death, do anything, but get that man. I'll be right out!' He hung up the phone.

        By instinct he jerked open the bottom desk drawer to get his service pistol. A pile of brown rust filled the new leather holster. He swore and leaped up.

175   On the way out of the office he grabbed a chair. It's wood, he thought. Good old-fashioned wood, good old-fashioned maple. He hurled it against the wall twice, and it broke. Then he seized one of the legs, clenched it hard in his fist, his face bursting red, the breath snorting in his nostrils, his mouth wide. He struck the palm of his hand with the leg of the chair, testing it. 'All right, God damn it, come on!'

180   he cried.

        He rushed out, yelling, and slammed the door.

Ray Bradbury

primordial: from the beginning of time
ochre: earth-coloured

Questions

7 What does the Official want the doctor to do?

8 What does he want the guard to do?

9 Why does the Official break up a chair?

10 This is the end of the story. What do you think could happen next?

Overview

The story is ...
Look at the following statements which try to sum up the story. Rank them in order with the best one first. Say why you have put them in this order.

A The story is about war.
B The story is about fear.
C The story is about dreams.
D The story is about the status quo.

What other statement could you make about the story? Add at least one more 'The story is about ...' sentence of your own.

Titles
One of the five titles below is the title that Ray Bradbury gave to his story.
Which one would you have chosen? Why?

- The Official View
- Rust
- A Piece of Wood
- Peace Panic
- Sixteen Years

Create another title for the story and explain why you chose it.

The Official

Summing him up
Look at these views of the Official in this story.

A The Official is basically sympathetic to the young sergeant.
B The Official has no interest in the young sergeant.
C The Official is essentially interested in his job.
D The Official is essentially interested in war continuing.
E The Official is frightened by the thought of peace.

1 How true is each of these views? Find evidence for your opinions.
2 Choose the view that you think sums up the Official best of all. Say why you have chosen it.
3 Write your own 'The Official is ...' sentence.

His language
The Official talks a good deal in this story. The way he speaks changes dramatically at a particular moment in the story.

1 When does this happen?
2 What changes can you see in his speech before and after this point?
3 How does this change in language reflect a change of attitude?
4 What do you learn about the Official from his use of language?

Writing about the story

1 Look back over the work you have done about the Official. Think about these points:

- what attitudes towards war, society, and human nature does he represent?
- what other aspects to his make-up does the story present?
- how are these represented by the way he speaks and acts?
- how does the author want us to respond to him?

Now write two or three paragraphs describing the character of the Official and his role in the story.

2 'Ray Bradbury's story gives a clear view of what he thinks about both war and human nature.'

- To what extent do you agree with that statement?
- What gives you a sense of how the writer feels?
- What makes the story either successful or unsuccessful in your eyes?

Try to make specific reference to the text itself wherever you can.

This can and normally should include quotation. However, do not copy out great chunks of the story to fill up space when you could be thinking and writing about the story itself.

Comparison

The young sergeant in Ray Bradbury's story and the blind man in Kate Chopin's story on page 105 are both outsiders. The ways that the two characters are presented are often quite different.

Kate Chopin provides a description of a street and what happens on that street. Ray Bradbury's story has a large amount of dialogue. Look back at both stories and make notes about how each story gives you a sense of the characters' isolation from the rest of society.

When your notes are complete, write a comparison of the lives and the situations of the two characters. Try to make it clear how the two writers create images of the characters in our minds.

Your own writing

Ray Bradbury's story is one of those which asks one of the great 'What if ...?' questions. Brainstorm one or more of these 'What ifs?' and make notes on the ideas you generate.

- What if school was voluntary?
- What if there was no school at all?
- What if there were no cars?
- What if there was no television?
- What if all criminals could be automatically caught?
- What if young people grew up together without their parents?
- What if there were no politicians?

Write your own story in which someone has the power to make one of these things happen or one of them has happened. Alternatively, make up your own 'What if ?', and write a story based on it.

B12 Doris and Graham

See: **A20** Character (p62) ● **A23** Dialogue in literature (p74)

The main texts in this unit are the openings of two television plays by Alan Bennett. They come from a series of half-hour plays called 'Talking Heads' which are monologues – long speeches for just one character.

As you read the scripts, try to hear each character speaking. There are questions at different points to help you do this.

Doris

Doris is in her seventies and the play is set in the living-room and hallway of her semi-detached house. She is sitting slightly awkwardly on a low chair and rubbing her leg. Morning.

It's such a silly thing to have done.

5   *Pause*

I should never have tried to dust. Zulema says to me every time she comes, 'Doris. Do not attempt to dust. The dusting is my department. That's what the council pay me for. You are now a lady of leisure. Your dusting
10   days are over.' Which would be all right provided she did dust. But Zulema doesn't dust. She half-dusts. I know when a place isn't clean.

Preparation

Before you turn over!

1 What do you think is the 'silly thing to have done'?
2 Who do you think Zulema might be?
3 What is your first impression of Doris? What might her voice sound like?

When she's going she says, 'Doris. I don't want to hear that you've been touching the Ewbank. The Ewbank is out of bounds.' I
15 said, 'I could just run round with it now and again.' She said, 'You can't run anywhere. You're on trial here.' I said, 'What for?' She said, 'For being on your own. For not behaving sensibly. For not acting like a woman of seventy-five who has a pacemaker and dizzy spells and doesn't have the sense she was born with.'

Ewbank: a type of carpet cleaner

20 I said, 'Yes, Zulema.' She says, 'What you don't understand, Doris, is that I am the only person that stands between you and Stafford House. I have to report on you. The Welfare say to me every time, "Well, Zulema, how is she coping? Wouldn't she be better off in Stafford House?"'

25 I said, 'They don't put people in Stafford House just for running round with the Ewbank.' 'No,' she says. 'They bend over backwards to keep you in your own home. But, Doris, you've got to meet them half-way. You're seventy-five. Pull your horns in. You don't have to swill the flags. You don't have to clean the bath. Let the dirt wait. It
30 won't kill you. I'm here every week.'

swill the flags: wash down the flagstones (stone used to make the path)

I was glad when she'd gone, dictating. I sat for a bit looking up at me and Wilfred on the wedding photo. And I thought, 'Well, Zulema, I bet you haven't dusted the top of that.' I used to be able to reach only I can't now. So I got the buffet and climbed up. And
35 she hadn't. Thick with dust. Home help. Home hindrance. You're better off doing it yourself. And I was just wiping it over when, oh hell, the flaming buffet went over.

buffet: small stool (usually for feet)

Pause

You feel such a fool. I can just hear Zulema. 'Well, Doris, I did tell you.' Only I think I'm all right. My leg's a bit numb but I've managed to get back on the chair. I'm just going to sit and come round a bit. Shakes you up, a fall.

Pause

Shan't let on I was dusting.

She shoves the duster down the side of the chair.

Dusting is forbidden.

She looks down at the wedding photo on the floor.

Cracked the photo. We're cracked, Wilfred.

Pause

The gate's open again. I thought it had blown shut, only now it's blown open. Bang bang bang all morning, it'll be bang bang bang all afternoon.

Dogs coming in, all sorts. You see Zulema should have closed that, only she didn't.

Pause

Preparation

4 What impression do you get of the relationship between Doris and Zulema?

■ What does Doris think of Zulema?
■ What do you suppose Zulema thinks of Doris?

5 What is Stafford House and what part does it play in the conversations the two of them have?
6 What other information are we given on these two pages about Doris's earlier life?

The sneck's loose, that's the root cause of it. It's wanted doing for years. I kept saying to Wilfred, 'When are you going to get round to that gate?' But oh no. It was always the same refrain. 'Don't worry, Mother. I've got it on my list.' I never saw no list. He had no list. I was the one with the list. He'd no system at all, Wilfred. 'When I get a minute, Doris.' Well, he's got a minute now, bless him.

Pause

Feels funny this leg. Not there.

65 *Pause*

Some leaves coming down now. I could do with trees if they didn't have leaves, going up and down the path. Zulema won't touch them. Says if I want leaves swept I've to contact the Parks Department.

70   I wouldn't care if they were my leaves. They're not my leaves. They're next-door's leaves. We don't have any leaves. I know that for a fact. We've only got the one little bush and it's an evergreen, so I'm certain they're not my leaves. Only other folks won't know that. They see the bush and they see the path and they think,

75 'Them's her leaves.' Well, they're not.

    I ought to put a note on the gate. 'Not my leaves.' Not my leg either, the way it feels. Gone to sleep.

Alan Bennett: *A Cream Cracker under the Settee*

sneck: latch

refrain: chorus, reply

7 What do we learn about her feelings towards Wilfred?

8 How do you imagine Doris gets on with her neighbours?

- What does she think of them?
- What do they think of her?

Graham

Graham is a mild, middle-aged man. The play is set in his bedroom, a small room with one window and one door. It is furnished with a single bed, a wardrobe, two chairs and nothing much else.

I'd just taken her tea up this morning when she said, 'Graham, I think the world of you.' I said, 'I think the world of you.' And she said, 'That's all right then.' I said, 'What's brought this on?' She said, 'Nothing. This tea looks strong, pull the curtains.' Of course I knew what had brought it on. She said, 'I wouldn't like you to think you're not Number One.' So I said, 'Well, you're Number One with me too. Give me your teeth. I'll swill them.'

swill: rinse, clean

What it was, we'd had a spot of excitement yesterday: we ran into a bit of Mother's past. I said to her, 'I didn't know you had a past. I thought I was your past.' She said, 'You?' I said, 'Well, we go back a long way. How does he fit in vis-à-vis Dad?' She laughed. 'Oh, he was pre-Dad.' I said, 'Pre-Dad? I'm surprised you remember him, you don't remember to switch your blanket off.' She said, 'That's different. His name's Turnbull.' I said, 'I know. He said.'

vis-à-vis: (say veez-a-vee) – in relation to

Preparation

1 This short section tells us a certain amount about two characters and their relationship. What do we learn for a fact?
2 It also hints at what happened yesterday. What clues are we given about this and what do you understand from them?
3 What are your first impressions of Graham?

I'd parked her by the war memorial on her usual seat while I went and got some reading matter. Then I waited while she went and spent a penny in the disabled toilet. She's not actually disabled, her memory's bad, but she says she prefers their toilets because you get more elbow room. She always takes for ever, diddling her hands and what not, and when she eventually comes back it turns out she's been chatting to the attendant. I said, 'What about?' She said, 'Hanging. She was in favour of stiffer penalties for minor offences and I thought, "Well, we know better, our Graham and me." I wish you'd been there, love; you could have given her the statistics, where are we going for our tea?'

diddling: fussing over

The thing about Mam is that though she's never had a proper education, she's picked up enough from me to be able to hold her own in discussions about up-to-the-minute issues like the environment and the colour problem, and for a woman of her age and background she has a very liberal slant. She'll look at my *Guardian* and she actually thinks for herself. Doctor Chaudhury said to me, 'Full marks, Graham. The best way to avoid a broken hip is to have a flexible mind. Keep up the good work.'

They go mad round the war memorial so when we cross over I'll generally slip my arm through hers until we're safely across, only once we're on the pavement she'll postpone letting it go, because once upon a time we got stopped by one of these questionnaire women who reckons to take us for husband and wife. I mean, Mam's got white hair. She was doing this dodge and I said, 'Mam, let go of my arm.' I didn't really wrench it, only next thing I knew she's flat on the pavement. I said, 'Oh my God, Mother.'

People gather round and I pick up her bag, and she sits up and says, 'I've laddered both my stockings.' I said, 'Never mind your stockings, what about your pelvis?' She says, 'It's these bifocals. They tell you not to look down. I was avoiding some sick.' Somebody says, 'That's a familiar voice,' and there's a little fellow bending over her, green trilby hat, shorty raincoat. 'Hello,' he says, 'remember me?'

pelvis: hip bone
bifocals: glasses which combine two lenses, one for close vision and one for looking further away

Well, she doesn't remember people, I know for a fact because she swore me down she'd never met Joy Buckle, who teaches Flowers in Felt and Fabric at my day centre. I said, 'You have met Joy, you knitted her a tea cosy.' That's all she can knit, tea cosies. And bed socks. Both outmoded articles. I said to her, 'Branch out. If you can knit tea cosies you can knit skiing hats.' She says, 'Well, I will.' Only I have to stand over her or else she'll still leave a hole for the spout. 'Anyway,' I said, 'you do remember Joy because you said she had some shocking eyebrows.' She said, 'I hope you didn't tell her that.' I said, 'Of course I didn't.' She said, 'Well, I don't remember.' And that's the way she is, she doesn't remember and here's this little fellow saying, 'Do you remember me?' So I said, 'No she won't. Come on, Mother. Let's get you up.'

outmoded: out of fashion

Preparation

4 Why did Graham stop his mother holding onto his arm? What does this tell you about him and her?
5 What further information do you get about Graham's way of life with his mother?
6 Is there any other information about Graham's life and character?

Only she says, 'Remember you? Of course. It's Frank Turnbull. It
must be fifty years.' He said, 'Fifty-two. Filey 1934.' She said, 'Sea-
Crest.' He said, 'No sand in the bedrooms.' And they both cracked out
laughing.

Meanwhile she's still stuck on the cold pavement. I said, 'Come
along, Mother. We don't want piles.' Only he butts in again. He says,
'With respect, it's advisable not to move a person until it's been
ascertained no bones are broken. I was in the St John's Ambulance
Brigade.' 'Yes,' said Mother, 'and who did you learn your bandaging
on?' And they both burst out laughing again. He had on these bright
yellow gloves, could have been a bookie.

Eventually, I get my arms round her waist and hoist her up, only
his lordship's no help as he claims to have a bad back. When I've
finally got her restored to the perpendicular she introduces him. 'This
is Frank Turnbull, a friend of mine from the old days.' What old days?
First time I knew there were any old days. Turns out he's a gents'
outfitter, semi-retired, shop in Bradford and some sort of outlet in
Morecambe. I thought, 'Well, that accounts for the yellow gloves.'

Straight off he takes charge. He says, 'What you need now, Vera, is
a cup of coffee.' I said, 'Well, we were just going for some tea, weren't
we, Mother?' Vera! Her name's not Vera. She's never been called Vera.
My Dad never called her Vera, except just once, when they were
wheeling him into the theatre. Vera. 'Right,' he says, 'follow me.' And
puts his arm through hers. 'Careful,' she says. 'You'll make my boy
friend jealous.' I didn't say anything.

Pause

cracked out: burst out

ascertained: made sure

perpendicular: vertical, upright

Now the café we generally patronise is just that bit different. It's plain but it's classy, no cloths on the tables, the menu comes on a little slate and the waitresses wear their own clothes and look as if they're doing it just for the fun of it. The stuff's all home-made and we're both big fans of the date and walnut bread. I said, 'This is the place.' Mr Turnbull goes straight past. 'No,' he says, 'I know somewhere, just opened. Press on.' Now, if there's one thing Mother and me are agreed on it's that red is a common colour. And the whole place is done out in red. Lampshades red. Waitresses in red. Plates red, and on the tables those plastic sauce things got up to look like tomatoes. Also red. And when I look there's a chip in the sugar. I thought, 'Mother won't like this.' 'Oh,' she says, 'this looks cheerful, doesn't it, Graham?' I said, 'There's a chip in the sugar.'

Alan Bennett: *A Chip in the Sugar*

Preparation

7 What picture do we have of Frank?

- What facts are given?
- How does Graham react to him?
- How does his mother react to the meeting?

8 What do we learn about Frank's previous relationship with Graham's mother?
9 Does Graham's description of the café add to our picture of him?

Practice

Getting the voice

If you have read with your imagination as well as your intelligence, you should by now be able to 'hear' the voices of the two characters.

1 Choose one of them.
2 Select a section of about ten lines to work on.
3 Practise reading it aloud. Think about:

- accent
- rhythm and tempo
- pauses.

If possible, work with a partner, so that you can listen to each other and give each other comments and advice.

Director's cut

If you were directing one of these scenes, how would you try to make it effective?

1 Choose one of the scenes.
2 Make notes on these points:

- what the character might wear
- how they might move
- how the lines should be spoken
- what the setting might look like.

A: Comparing the scenes

Write a comparison of these two opening scenes by Alan Bennett and compare them.

Preparation

Think about these points and make notes on them:

- The impression you have of the main character.
- The way other (offstage) characters are portrayed.
- The way the main character uses language.
- The humour and the tensions in each opening.
- The potential for developing the story.
- What is effective about each of them as the opening of a play.
- Which play you would be more interested in seeing in full as a result of the first scene.
- Any other points that struck you as you read the scenes.

Look at the notes you have made and plan the best order in which to present them.

Writing

Now write your comparison. This is quite a detailed and complicated piece of writing, so you may find it helps to write a rough draft first.

B: Graham's story, Doris's story

Choose one of the two scenes and write your own version of the next section.

Preparation

Think about these points and jot down the ideas you have:

- How might Graham or Doris continue their story?
- What might they reveal?
- If the next scene were an hour/day/week later, what might have happened?

Writing

Now write your scene. Try to keep the character and the language of Graham or Doris consistent with the scene you have studied.

C: Your own character

Create a monologue for your own choice of character.

1 Choose a character. Here are some ideas:

  - a new caretaker
  - a dentist
  - a young person newly arrived in the area
  - a grandparent who has recently moved in with their family.

2 Think about what kind of person your character is and how he or she speaks.
3 Try writing a few lines of monologue, to get the feel of your character.
4 Think of something that has happened which could form the starting point of your monologue.
5 Now write your monologue.

D: Monologue to dialogue

Choose one of the two plays and write a new scene for it:

Doris

What might happen when Zulema next visits Doris? Write the dialogue that they might have. Look back at what Doris thinks and what she tells us of their last conversation to give yourself ideas.

Graham

What would the scene have been like in the café between Graham, his mum Vera and Frank Turnbull? Write the scene as you think it might have happened.

Look back at the scene you have studied to find a sense of how the three characters behave together.

TONY KYTES,
THE ARCH-DECEIVER

See: **A20** Character (p62) ● **A21** Action (p66)
● **A5** Reading 'between the lines' (p17)

Thomas Hardy (1840–1928) was the first major writer to focus on the countryside and on rural characters. His novels, stories and poems were set in the area he called 'Wessex', present-day Dorset, Wiltshire and Hampshire. Hardy wrote at a time when life was changing in some areas for the first time in centuries. Railways were spreading rapidly as the industrial revolution started to affect the whole population. Many people were beginning to leave the countryside for jobs in the town and to move from job to job. It was also a period when belief in Christianity was under pressure. Many people, including Hardy himself, experienced a loss of faith. These changes created a sense of challenge to traditional standards which was often reflected in Hardy's novels and short stories. His writing was praised by some critics for its realism and harshly condemned by others who accused him of attacking traditional moral standards.

One series of stories was written as if they were tales that were told on a horse-drawn cart returning from town to the village of Longpuddle. The stories begin in response to the interest of someone who is returning to the village after 35 years and wants to know what has happened. The driver of the cart tells the first tale which recounts what happened to Tony Kytes.

I shall never forget Tony's face. 'Twas a little, round, firm, tight face, with a seam here and there left by the smallpox, but not enough to hurt his looks in a woman's eye, though he'd had it baddish when he was a boy. So very serious looking and unsmiling 'a was, that young man, that it really seemed as if he
5   couldn't laugh at all without great pain to his conscience. He looked very hard at a small speck in your eye when talking to 'ee. And there was no more sign of a whisker or beard on Tony Kytes's face than on the palm of my hand. He used to sing 'The Tailor's Breeches' with a religious manner, as if it were a hymn:—
10   O the petticoats went off, and the breeches they went on!
and all the rest of the scandalous stuff. He was quite the women's favourite, and in return for their likings he loved 'em in shoals.

shoals: large numbers

But in course of time Tony got fixed down to one in particular, Milly
Richards, a nice, light, small, tender little thing; and it was soon said that they
were engaged to be married. One Saturday he had been to market to do
business for his father, and was driving home the waggon in the afternoon.
When he reached the foot of the very hill we shall be going over in ten minutes
who should he see waiting for him at the top but Unity Sallet, a handsome girl,
one of the young women he'd been very tender towards before he'd got
engaged to Milly.

As soon as Tony came up to her she said, 'My dear Tony, will you give me a
lift home?'

'That I will, darling,' said Tony. 'You don't suppose I could refuse 'ee?'

She smiled a smile, and up she hopped, and on drove Tony.

'Tony,' she says, in a sort of tender chide, 'why did ye desert me for that
other one? In what is she better than I? I should have made 'ee a finer wife,
and a more loving one, too. 'Tisn't girls that are so easily won at first that are
the best. Think how long we've known each other – ever since we were children
almost – now haven't we, Tony?'

chide: criticism, rebuke

'Yes, that we have,' says Tony, a-struck with the truth o't.

'And you've never seen anything in me to complain of, have ye, Tony? Now tell the truth to me!'

'I never have, upon my life,' says Tony.

'And – can you say I'm not pretty, Tony? Now look at me!'

He let his eyes light upon her for a long while. 'I really can't,' says he. 'In fact, I never knowed you was so pretty before!'

'Prettier than she?'

What Tony would have said to that nobody knows for before he could speak, what should he see ahead, over the hedge past the turning, but a feather he knew well – the feather in Milly's hat – she to whom he had been thinking of putting the question as to giving out the banns that very week.

banns: legal announcement of a wedding

'Unity,' says he, as mild as he could, 'here's Milly coming. Now I shall catch it mightily if she sees 'ee riding here with me; and if you get down she'll be turning the corner in a moment, and, seeing 'ee in the road, she'll know we've been corning on together. Now, dearest Unity, will ye, to avoid all unpleasantness, which I know ye can't bear any more than I, will ye lie down in the back part of the waggon, and let me cover you over with the tarpaulin till Milly has passed? It will all be done in a minute. Do! – and I'll think over what we've said, and perhaps I shall put a loving question to you after all, instead of to Milly. 'Tisn't true that it is all settled between her and me.'

tarpaulin: large canvas sheet to cover a wagon

Well, Unity Sallet agreed, and lay down at the back end of the waggon, and Tony covered her over, so that the waggon seemed to be empty but for the loose tarpaulin: and then he drove on to meet Milly.

'My dear Tony!' cries Milly, looking up with a little pout at him as he came near. 'How long you've been coming home! Just as if I didn't live at Upper Longpuddle at all! And I've come to meet you as you asked me to do, and to ride back with you, and talk over our future home – since you asked me, and I promised. But I shouldn't have come else, Mr Tony!'

'Ay, my dear, I did ask 'ee – to be sure I did, now I think of it – but I had quite forgot it. To ride back with me, did you say, dear Milly?'

'Well, of course! What can I do else? Surely you don't want me to walk, now I've come all this way?'

'O no, no! I was thinking you might be going on to town to meet your mother. I saw her there – and she looked as if she might be expecting 'ee.'

'O no; she's just home. She came across the fields, and so got back before you.'

'Ah! I didn't know that,' says Tony. And there was no help for it but to take her up beside him.

They talked on very pleasantly, and looked at the trees, and beasts, and birds, and insects, and at the ploughmen at work in the fields, till presently who should they see looking out of the upper window of a house that stood beside the road they were following, but Hannah Jolliver, another young beauty of the place at that time, and the very first woman that Tony had fallen in love with – before Milly and before Unity, in fact – the one that he had almost arranged to marry instead of Milly. She was a much more dashing girl than Milly Richards, though he'd not thought much of her of late. The house Hannah was looking from was her aunt's.

dashing: smart and lively

'My dear Milly – my coming wife, as I may call 'ee,' says Tony in his modest way, and not so loud that Unity could overhear, 'I see a young woman

80 a-looking out of the window, who I think may accost me. The fact is, Milly, she had a notion that I was wishing to marry her, and since she's discovered I've promised another, and a prettier than she, I'm rather afeard of her temper if she sees us together. Now, Milly, would you do me a favour – my coming wife, as I may say?'

85 'Certainly, dearest Tony,' says she.

'Then would ye creep under the empty sacks just here in the front of the waggon, and hide there out of sight till we've passed the house? She hasn't seen us yet. You see, we ought to live in peace and goodwill since 'tis almost Christmas, and 'twill prevent angry passions rising, which we always should

90 do.'

'I don't mind, to oblige you, Tony,' Milly said; and though she didn't care much about doing it, she crept under, and crouched down just behind the seat, Unity being snug at the other end. So they drove on till they got near the road-side cottage. Hannah had soon seen him coming, and waited at the

95 window, looking down upon him. She tossed her head a little disdainful and smiled off-hand.

'Well, aren't you going to be civil enough to ask me to ride home with you!' she says, seeing that he was for driving past with a nod and a smile.

'Ah, to be sure! What was I thinking of?' said Tony, in a flutter. 'But you

100 seem as if you was staying at your aunt's?'

'No, I am not,' she said. 'Don't you see I have my bonnet and jacket on? I have only called to see her on my way home. How can you be so stupid, Tony?'

'In that case ah – of course you must come along wi' me,' says Tony, feeling a dim sort of sweat rising up inside his clothes. And he reined in the horse,

105 and waited till she'd come downstairs, and then helped her up beside him, her feet outside. He drove on again, his face as long as a face that was a round one by nature well could be. Hannah looked round sideways into his eyes. 'This is nice, isn't it, Tony?' she says. 'I like riding with you.' Tony looked back into her eyes. 'And I with you,' he said after a while. In short, having considered

110 her, he warmed up, and the more he looked at her the more he liked her, till he couldn't for the life of him think why he had ever said a word about marriage to Milly or Unity while Hannah Jolliver was in question. So they sat a little closer and closer, their feet upon the foot-board and their shoulders touching, and Tony thought over and over again how handsome Hannah was. He spoke

115 tenderer and tenderer, and called her 'dear Hannah' in a whisper at last.

'You've settled it with Milly by this time, I suppose?' said she.

'N – no, not exactly.'

'What? How low you talk, Tony.'

'Yes – I've a kind of hoarseness. I said, not exactly.'

120 'I suppose you mean to?'

'Well, as to that.' His eyes rested on her face and hers on his. He wondered how he could have been such a fool as not to follow up Hannah. 'My sweet Hannah!' he bursts out, taking her hand, not being really able to help it, and forgetting Milly and Unity, and all the world besides. 'Settled it? I don't think I

125 have!'

accost: stop with a greeting (often a sharp greeting)

disdainful: scornful

civil: polite

'Hark!' says Hannah.

'What?' says Tony, letting go her hand.

'Surely I heard a sort of little screaming squeak under those sacks? Why, you've been carrying corn, and there's mice in this waggon, I declare!' She began to haul up the tails of her gown.

'O no, 'tis the axle,' said Tony in an assuring way. 'It do go like that sometimes in dry weather.'

'Perhaps it was … Well, now, to be quite honest, dear Tony, do you like her better than me? Because – because, although I've held off so independent, I'll own at last that I do like 'ee, Tony, to tell the truth; and I wouldn't say no if you asked me – you know what.' Tony was so won over by this pretty offering mood of a girl who had been quite the reverse (Hannah had a backward way with her at times, if you can mind) that he just glanced behind, and then whispered very soft, 'I haven't quite promised her, and I think I can get out of it, and ask you that question you speak of.'

'Throw over Milly? – all to marry me! How delightful!' broke out Hannah, quite loud, clapping her hands.' At this there was a real squeak – an angry, spiteful squeak, and afterward a long moan, as if something had broke its heart, and a movement of the empty sacks.

assuring: comforting and confident (reassuring)

a backward way: a reserved, reluctant way, not quick to trust someone

145   'Something's there!' said Hannah, starting up.

'It's nothing. Really,' says Tony in a soothing voice, and praying inwardly for a way out of this. 'I wouldn't tell 'ee at first, because I wouldn't frighten 'ee. But, Hannah, I've really a couple of ferrets in a bag under there, for rabbiting, and they quarrel sometimes. I don't wish it knowed, as 'twould be called poaching. Oh, they

150   can't get out, bless 'ee – you are quite safe! And – and – what a fine day it is, isn't it, Hannah, for this time of year? Be you going to market next Saturday? How is your aunt now?'And so on, says Tony, to keep her from talking any more about love in Milly's hearing. But he found his work cut out for him, and wondering again how he should get out of this ticklish business, he looked about for a chance. Nearing

155   home he saw his father in a field not far off, holding up his hand as if he wished to speak to Tony

'Would you mind taking the reins a moment, Hannah,' he said, much relieved, 'while I go and find out what father wants?'

She consented, and away he hastened into the field, only too glad to get

160   breathing time. He found that his father was looking at him with rather a stern eye.

'Come, come, Tony,' says old Mr. Kytes, as soon as his son was alongside him, 'this won't do, you know.'

'What?' says Tony.

'Why, if you mean to marry Milly Richards, do it, and there's an end o't. But don't

165   go driving about the country with Jolliver's daughter and making a scandal. I won't have such things done.'

'I only asked her – that is, she asked me, to ride home.'

'She? Why, now, if it had been Milly, 'twould have been quite proper; but you and Hannah Jolliver going about by yourselves.'

170   'Milly's there, too, father.'

'Milly? Where?'

'Under the corn-sacks! Yes, the truth is, father, I've got rather into a nunnywatch, I'm afeard! Unity Sallet is there, too, yes, at the other end, under the tarpaulin. All three are in that waggon, and what to do with 'em I know no more than the dead!

175   The best plan is, as I'm thinking, to speak out loud and plain to one of 'em before the rest, and that will settle it; not but what 'twill cause 'em to kick up a bit of a miff, for certain. Now which would you marry, father, if you was in my place?'

'Whichever of 'em did not ask to ride with thee.'

'That was Milly, I'm bound to say, as she only mounted by my invitation. But

180   Milly.'

'Then stick to Milly, she's the best – But look at that!' … His father pointed toward the waggon. 'She can't hold that horse in. You shouldn't have left the reins in her hands. Run on and take the horse's head, or there'll be some accident to them maids!'

185   Tony's horse, in fact, in spite of Hannah's tugging at the reins, had started on his way at a brisk walking pace, being very anxious to get back to the stable, for he had had a long day out. Without another word Tony rushed away from his father to overtake the horse. Now of all things that could have happened to wean him from Milly there was nothing so powerful as his father's recommending her. No; it could

190   not be Milly, after all. Hannah must be the one, since he could not marry all three as he longed to do. This he thought while running after the waggon. But queer things were happening inside.

this ticklish business: awkward or difficult business requiring tact

nunnywatch: tangled mess

miff: short outburst of temper

maids: girls

B13 Tony Kytes, the arch-deceiver

It was, of course, Milly who had screamed under the sack-bags, being obliged to let off her bitter rage and shame in that way at what Tony was saying, and never daring to show, for very pride and dread o' being laughed at, that she was in hiding. She became more and more restless, and in twisting herself about, what did she see but another woman's foot and white stocking close to her head. It quite frightened her, not knowing that Unity Sallet was in the waggon likewise. But after the fright was over she determined to get to the bottom of all this, and she crept and crept along the bed of the waggon, under the tarpaulin, like a snake, when lo and behold she came face to face with Unity.

'Well, if this isn't disgraceful!' says Milly in a raging whisper to Unity.

''Tis,' says Unity, 'to see you hiding in a young man's waggon like this, and no great character belonging to either of ye!'

'Mind what you are saying!' replied Milly, getting louder. 'I am engaged to be married to him, and haven't I a right to be here? What right have you, I should like to know? What has he been promising you? A pretty lot of nonsense, I expect! But what Tony says to other women is all mere wind, and no concern to me!'

'Don't you be too sure!' says Unity. 'He's going to have Hannah, and not you, nor me either; I could hear that.' Now at these strange voices sounding from under the cloth Hannah was thunderstruck a'most into a swound; and it was just at this time that the horse moved on. Hannah tugged away wildly, not knowing what she was doing; and as the quarrel rose louder and louder, Hannah got so horrified that she let go the reins altogether. The horse went on at his own pace, and coming to the corner where we turn round to drop down the hill to Lower Longpuddle he turned too quick, the off wheels went up the bank, the waggon rose sideways till it was quite on edge upon the near axles, and out rolled the three maidens into the road in a heap. The horse looked round and stood still. When Tony came up, frightened and breathless, he was relieved enough to see that neither of his darlings was hurt, beyond a few scratches from the brambles of the hedge. But he was rather alarmed when he heard how they were going on at one another.

'Don't ye quarrel, my dears – don't ye!' says he, taking off his hat out of respect to 'em. And then he would have kissed them all round, as fair and square as a man could, but they were in too much of a taking to let him, and screeched and sobbed till they was quite spent.

'Now I'll speak out honest, because I ought to,' says Tony, as soon as he could get heard. 'And this is the truth,' says he. 'I've asked Hannah to be mine, and she is willing, and we are going to put up the banns next –'

Tony had not noticed that Hannah's father was coming up behind, nor had he noticed that Hannah's face was beginning to bleed from the scratch of a bramble. Hannah had seen her father, and had run to him, crying worse than ever.

'My daughter is not willing, sir!' says Mr. Jolliver hot and strong. 'Be you willing, Hannah? I ask ye to have spirit enough to refuse him, if yer virtue is left to 'ee and you run no risk?'

'She's as sound as a bell for me, that I'll swear!' says Tony, flaring up. 'And so's the others, come to that, though you may think it an unusual thing in me!'

thunderstruck: stunned, amazed, confused

swound: a faint

'I have spirit, and I do refuse him!' says Hannah, partly because her father was there, and partly, too, in a tantrum because of the discovery, and the scar that might be left on her face. 'Little did I think when I was so

245 soft with him just now that I was talking to such a false deceiver!'

'What, you won't have me, Hannah?' says Tony, his jaw hanging down like a dead man's.

'Never – I would sooner marry no – nobody at all!' she gasped

250 out, though with her heart in her throat, for she would not have refused Tony if he had asked her quietly, and her father had not been there, and her face had not been scratched by the bramble. And having said that, away she walked upon her father's arm, thinking and hoping he would ask her again. Tony didn't know what to say next. Milly was sobbing

255 her heart out; but as his father had strongly recommended her he couldn't feel inclined that way. So he turned to Unity.

'Well, will you, Unity dear, be mine?' he says.

'Take her leavings? Not I!' says Unity. 'I'd scorn it!'

And away walks Unity Sallet likewise, though she looked back when she'd

260 gone some way, to see if he was following her. So there at last were left Milly and Tony by themselves, she crying in watery streams, and Tony looking like a tree struck by lightning.

'Well, Milly,' he says at last, going up to her, 'it do seem as if fate had ordained that it should be you and I, or nobody. And what must be must be,

265 I suppose. Hey, Milly?'

ordained: ordered, destined to be

'If you like, Tony. You didn't really mean what you said to them?'

'Not a word of it!' declares Tony, bringing down his fist upon his palm.

And then he kissed her, and put the waggon to rights, and they mounted together; and their banns were put up the very next Sunday. I was not able to

270 go to their wedding, but it was a rare party they had, by all account. Everyone in Longpuddle was there almost.

rare: outstanding

Thomas Hardy: *Tony Kytes, the Arch-deceiver*

Close reading

Make sure you refer closely to the text when you answer. Long quotations are not helpful but short appropriate ones will support a good answer.

1 What impression does the reader have of Tony Kytes from the first paragraph (lines 1 to 12)?

2 Look at the section in which Tony is with Unity Sallet before he meets Milly (lines 21 to 53). Complete these two statements.
'Unity Sallet encourages Tony's weak nature by ...'
'Tony is guilty of making the situation worse with Unity because ...'

3 Look at the section in which Tony is with Milly Richards before they arrive at the cottage of Hannah's aunt (lines 54 to 94).
What impression do you have of Milly's character?

4 Look at the section where Tony is with Hannah Jolliver up to the moment when he sees his father in a field (lines 94 to 156).
In what ways is Hannah different from Milly? Why does he encourage her in hopes of marriage?

5 Look at the section where Tony is with his father up to the point where he is running after the wagon (lines 161 to 192).
What clues are there about the relationship between father and son?

6 Look at the section where Tony makes the three proposals of marriage (lines 229 to 271). What do you discover about Hannah, Unity and Milly through this incident?
In what ways does it confirm or alter what you thought about them before this moment?

Character

There are four main characters in this story – Tony, Unity, Milly and Hannah.

1 Look at the words and phrases given below and discuss which apply to which characters and why. You may think that some apply to none of them and some apply to more than one.

easily swayed	unsure of their own mind
independent	foolish
difficult to please	short-tempered
easy to please	good-looking
smart	proud

2 Now think of as many phrases as you can of your own. Aim to have at least two or three for each character and an explanation of your choices.

3 Use a chart like this to record your ideas:

TONY	UNITY	MILLY
unsure of own mind – asks father who he should marry	proud – when Hannah rejects Tony she	

Extended response to reading: critical evaluation

4 Choose two of the four main characters in Hardy's story and discuss how they are portrayed in the story. Describe in detail their strengths and weaknesses, as you see them, using the character chart to help you.

You should refer to what happens in the story and what is said by them and about them in order to illustrate the points you are making. Your work will be improved by the use of short, relevant quotations. Conclude by stating how you responded to the character in the story.

Hardy's world

The world in which Thomas Hardy lived was described
very briefly in the introduction to this story. Look back at
the introduction and then consider three things.

a In what ways is the society in which Hardy lived
reflected in this story?

b In what ways is the world described in this story
different from our own?

c What aspects of Hardy's writing as shown here might
have given rise to the sharp criticism that eventually
led him to abandon novel and short story writing?

Practice

Coursework

Overall impression

The comic effect of Hardy's story depends on a
mixture of character, plot and a willingness to
surprise the moral expectations of society.

Write about the way you see this happening in
Tony Kytes, the arch-deceiver. You may like
to consider:

- the way Tony's 'weakness' lets the situation
develop
- the way each of the girls complicates the
situation
- the increasingly complicated situation in the cart
- the role of Tony's father
- the final scene with its three marriage proposals.

Mr Kytes

Imagine that Tony's father is talking to a close
friend about Tony and his escapade with Unity, Milly
and Hannah. He tells the story, paying particular
attention to his views of the characters of Tony and
the three girls. What does he say?

Scenes from a life

Most people enjoy talking about their own lives – things they remember, and things they would like to forget. This unit looks at writing about memories – pleasant and unpleasant. As you work through it you will read about other people's lives and write a series of short pieces of autobiography. All these will be in the form of a first draft. At the end of the unit there are suggestions for ways in which you can undertake a longer piece of writing.

See: ● **A13** Narrative (p39)
● **A14** Description (p42)
● **A15** Explanation (p46)
● **A23** Dialogue in literature (p74)

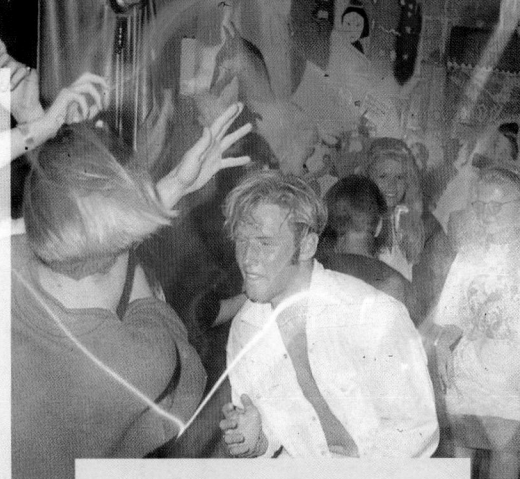

... My parents never let us have parties like that, but we did have one once when my mother was away. My mum had gone away to the caravan – that's what they did for their week's holiday – and I kept saying that I didn't want to go.
5   I was 15 and I didn't want to go off to a caravan, so she said she was going off on her own. I think my brother also stayed behind so she just took my younger sister. My elder sister must have been in London by then. Anyway, as soon as she was gone, I organised a party, the only party we ever had at
10 our house at that time. I had to bribe my brother not to tell. We got all the booze in and everything and moved all the furniture out of the way. Then at about 1 o'clock in the morning the police turned up looking for somebody. We saw them coming up the path, so what the fellas did was they
15 shoved all the beer bottles under the settee. We thought that you weren't allowed to drink at our age, even indoors, so we didn't want the police to see the beer. The fellas were hiding bottles everywhere and beer got spilled all over the place. Afterwards we couldn't get rid of the smell, and all the police
20 had come for was to get one of the girls. She'd told her mother she was going to a youth club and it was a bit late, so her mother had got them to look for her. That party went on until about 3 a.m.

Joan, talking about her life in Growing up in the 60s
by **Cecile Landau**

Thinking, talking

1   Is Joan's family life in the 1960s very different from yours?
    In what ways are her family different?
    In what ways are they like your family?

2   Do parties still cause disasters? Why?

3   What other areas of your life are likely to cause incidents ... disasters ... things that you cringe at or laugh about when you remember them?

I remember ...

Preparation

Brainstorming

Work in a group of three or four for this. Everyone in the group needs paper and something to write with.

What kinds of things do you remember from the last few years of life? What:

- public events
- pop songs and stars
- television programmes
- fashions
- toys

do you remember? And what else?

1 Everybody in the group just says whatever they remember and make notes.
2 No one disagrees, laughs or comments on what other people say.
3 No one starts having a conversation about something else.
4 Give yourselves three or four minutes and then look through your notes. If possible add some more.

Writing

Now write a group poem using your list. Each line begins 'I remember ...'

Joggers

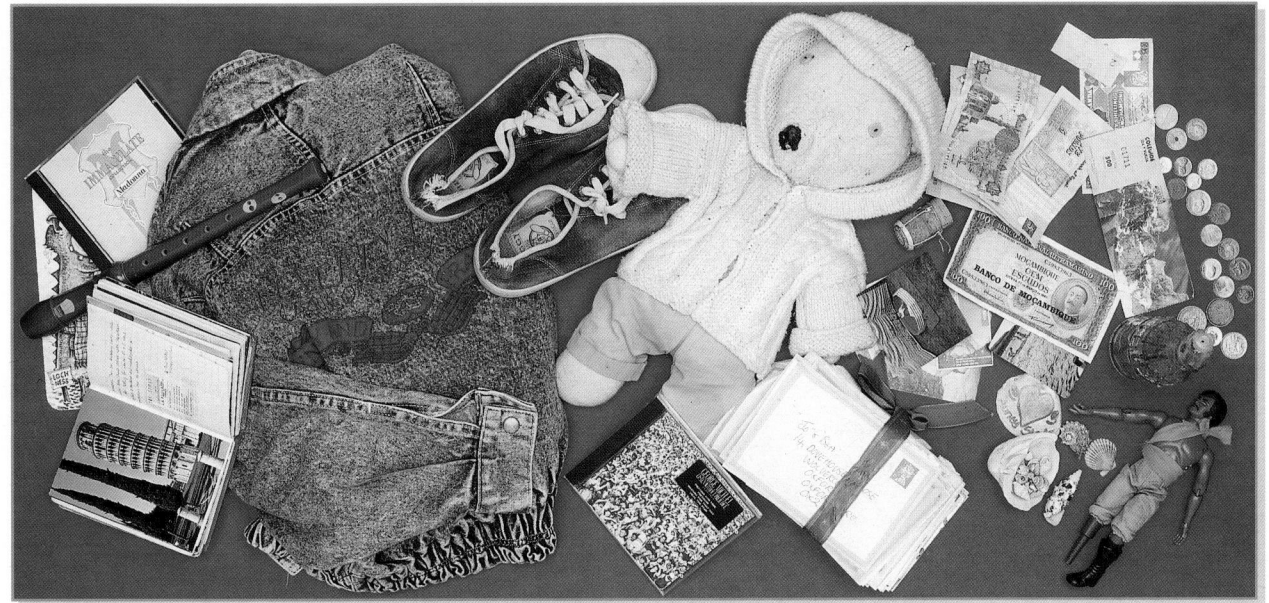

Old photographs, foreign coins, broken toys … Different things bring back different memories for different people. Collect together one or two things that bring back memories – happy or otherwise – and bring them to school.

Preparation

Pair work

Show each other your memory joggers and describe the memories they recall. Talking about them will bring back details that you had forgotten and may stir other memories, so make notes of what you remember.

Writing a poem

Use your notes to help you write a simple poem. Each verse starts with one line that describes the memory jogger. Then successive lines sketch in the memory that is jogged:

A torn postcard of Pevensey:
Running along the cliffs with Martin,
Catching my foot in a hidden tree root,
Gasping for breath with the pain.
Then realising I couldn't walk …
The long wait while Martin got help.

Practice

Coursework

Putting in the detail

By now you have spent quite a lot of time riffling through your memory and pulling out all sorts of odds and ends that were stored there. Now is the time to focus on one event and write about it in a little more detail. It may be something you have already mentioned in the writing you have done, or it may be something new.

1 Choose what you are going to write about.
2 Focus all your attention on that memory.
3 Write down quickly all the details that you can remember. Don't worry about writing complete sentences; that will come later.
4 Sort out the notes you have made and think about shaping them into a narrative that makes sense.
5 Now write your memory.

Standard Grade English – Credit

Family memories

Bill Bryden, the playwright and director, wrote a memoir of his childhood, which he called ''Member 'At? ' for a collection published by Save the Children. Bill spent his childhood in Greenock, on the Clyde estuary. In this extract, he uses dialogue to recapture the vividness of particular moments …

Holidays in Campbeltown. Auntie Tina, Anna, Jamie, Bunty Paterson. The sea. Waves. Being sick on the boat. 1949. Three hundred Greenockians spewing their rings up beyond Lochranza. But, 'Arrived safely. Weather fine. Wish you were here'. The mystery tour.

5   'Is it Clachan or Carradale?'
         'Cannae tell ye.'
         'Is it Clachan or Carradale?'
         'It's a mystery.'
         'Look! I went on "the mystery" on Monday night and that was Clachan.
10 I went on "the mystery" last night and that was Clachan as well. But, see Mrs Fielding! She went on "the mystery" on Tuesday and that was Carradale so I want tae know where "the mystery's" goin' the night?'
         'It wouldnae be a mystery then, would it?'
         'OK. Tell me it's no' goin' tae Clachan. I hate Clachan. Full o' midges.'
15   'Look, are you comin' or no?'
         'Och, passes the night.'
     The driver at that moment changed the solution to the mystery and took her to Clachan just for spite.
         How can I go back to Campbeltown? I want to take my children.
20 I probably won't. I'm sure it's too … changed.

The Coronation. One TV in Carwood Street. Jean Chambers. Number seven. The whole street for the whole day in a two room and kitchen. The fireworks at the end. A Duke of Norfolk production.
         'It was like VE Night.'
25   'Aye. She was lovely.'
         'We must get one.'
         'Sixty poun's a lotta money.'
         'You can rent it frae Clydesdale.'
         'Can ye?'
30   'Sure.'
         'Fourteen inch?'
         'Aye. It's that cheery. And there's Muffin the Mule for the weans.'
     The first night we got the television Leslie Mitchell exploded and no amount of banging brought him back to Alexandra Palace. My father who
35 was rarely furious near did his nut.
         'member 'at?

Bill Bryden: *'Member 'At?*

Preparation

Reading aloud

Work in a group of three for this.

There are parts of the extract where two voices are presented in conversation, almost like a play. The author's narration gives the background to each scene.

1 Cast the parts of narrator, first voice, second voice.

2 Read aloud the extract, treating it like a script:

NARRATOR: . . . The mystery tour.
FIRST VOICE: Is it Clachan or Carradale?
SECOND VOICE: Cannae tell ye.

3 Discuss how your performance can be improved and practise it until you are satisfied with it.

Conversations

What do your family sound like?

Think about some of the situations in which conversations take place and try writing up one or two typical examples.

Here are some possible subjects and scenes:

- the breakfast table
- which television programme to watch
- the time you have to be in at night
- the friends you keep
- the amount of money you get
- the state of your bedroom
- getting up in the morning
- helping with work in the house.

Charting a life

So far you have been looking at short episodes from your life. If your writing has been successful they will have been vividly remembered and recounted. Now the time has come to put them into a context: how do they fit into the pattern of your life as a whole?

One way of looking at this is to make a chart of your life so far. Draw up a detailed 'timetable' going right back to when you were born and continuing to the present day. Either devise your own way of doing this, or copy the example below:

Year	Where I lived	Milestones	Key memories
1993	53 Highburgh Road, Glasgow	We moved from Newton Stewart to Glasgow. I went to Dowanhill Primary School.	I hated it at first – it seemed so big. Everyone had their own friends. Lewis arrived and we became best mates. He came on holiday with us to Wigtownshire. I fell out of the boat when we were fishing.

Practice

Coursework

Writing

Choose an event that you think was important in your life.
You are going to write about it in a slightly different way.

Preparation

1 Focus all your attention on remembering the event you have chosen.
2 Write down quickly all the details that you can remember. Don't worry about writing complete sentences; that will come later.
3 Look at what you have written and think about why that event was important in your life. Write some more notes about this if necessary.

Writing

Now write an account of the event, but write it as if it had happened to someone else. Instead of writing *I*, write *she* or *he*.

Crafting a life

Writing a piece of autobiography takes as much skill and imagination as writing a piece of fiction. The following extracts introduce sections of autobiographical writing from a wide range of writers. Read them through at least twice, thinking about the pictures that the words suggest to you.

A

I sauntered slowly along the dusty road, kicking loose stones ahead of me. It was a warm day, and I felt as languid as the black and yellow bumble bee droning on the hedge beside me. I sat down on the side of the ditch and watched a ladybird crawl up my bare brown leg. I was on my way to spend a week with my grandmother and was reluctant to arrive.

Alice Taylor: *Country Days*

B

It is a bright summer day in 1947. My father, a fat, funny man with beautiful eyes and a subversive wit, is trying to decide which of his eight children he will take with him to the county fair. My mother, of course, will not go. She is knocked out from getting us ready: I hold my neck stiff against the pressure of her knuckles as she hastily completes the braiding and then beribboning of my hair.

Alice Walker: *In Search of Our Mothers' Gardens*

C

September. Towards the end of the afternoon of a day poised between late summer and early autumn. I sat in the garden beneath the magic apple tree. Below me, on the other side of the low stone wall, the countryside fell away, the meadows sloping down to the stream and the line of willow trees that stand beside it, and then rising gently up again to the far, high slope of the other side of the village.

Susan Hill: *Family*

D

My father had no time for contemplating the loveliness of his estate. He was far too busy running it. This was not made any easier by the fact that he had had absolutely no preparation for the task, being by both training and inclination a cavalry soldier. In my grandfather's time, nobody thought of teaching a boy how to manage his inheritance; if he was the eldest son, it was assumed that he would know how to act when the time came for him to succeed. I was too young to know how my father ran the estate, but where his children were concerned he was an implacable disciplinarian, dealing with us in a strictly military manner.

Christian Miller: *A Childhood in Scotland*

E

The old lady is seated at one end of the long table in the dining-room absorbed in some accounts, glasses perched on her nose. With the out-stretched forefinger of her left hand, circled by a large ring, she holds down the paper while with her right she is scratching some figures using an oversized pen.

Michael Jenkins: *A House in Flanders*

Responding

Now set out your response to the five extracts, using a table like this:

Extract	The picture it suggested	The way it is written
A	A dreamy, hot summer's day, during the school holidays. A young girl – perhaps eight or nine years old – is	Focuses on the writer's thoughts and feelings and physical sensations. Starts slowly, without explaining what is going on, and then

Practice

Viewpoint, focus, style

These writers all began with a similar intention: to describe as vividly as possible an event from their earlier lives. Yet they have all tackled it in very different ways. There are several different ways in which each writer's approach is individual:

■ each looks at the experience from a different viewpoint.
   (**A** looks at the experience as if they were still a child, while **D** is very much an adult remembering.)

■ each focuses on different aspects of the memory. (**C** describes the scene, while **E** is concerned with action.)

■ each presents the experience in a different way. (**E** is mysterious, while **B** is much more straightforward.)

■ each has a different voice.
   (Try reading them aloud and you will soon see this.)

Coursework

Bringing the strands together

If you have worked through this unit, you will have done a number of pieces of writing, all first drafts; of any or all of the following:

1 Group poem *I remember …* (page 166)
2 *Writing a poem* (p167)
3 *Putting in the detail* (p167)
4 *Conversations* (p169)
5 *Charting a life* (p170)

You can, if you wish, stop there. You have already had the opportunity to think, talk, and write about your life in a concentrated and interesting way. On the other hand, you could spend some more time bringing the strands together and thinking a bit more about the life you have been describing. Here are two ways in which you could do this:

1 Make a personal anthology of memories. Go through the writing you have done, redrafting it and polishing it up for other people to read. You may find that you have thought of other memories you wish to add. You might like to link the memories by a commentary or expanded chart like the one on page 170.
2 Use your first drafts as the raw material for one extended piece of writing. If you are going to do this, you will find it helpful to think back to your response to the texts on page 171 and the earlier work on this page.

HOT OFF THE PRESS

See: ● **A11** Making notes (p34)
● **A18** Writing a newspaper report (p56)
● **A19** Writing an article (p59)
● **B10** Media texts (p133)

Me? ... you're joking!

Most journalism done in school is either a class exercise or for a school publication. It is not often for a much wider readership. However, some newspapers link up with schools to produce news and features that are prepared by pupils. Like any other journalist, you may not get very much warning.

Richard Collins and Angela Coughlin arrived in school as usual one Monday morning expecting to work their normal timetable. Instead, they found the Head of English waiting for them with the 'good' news that they were going to be journalists for the morning. They had just over ninety minutes to prepare to interview a world champion.

'It all happened so fast. You didn't have enough time to think'

'The most difficult thing was coming up with the right sorts of questions'

The kind of writing Richard and Angela were being asked to do is called a feature interview. In this unit we look at some of the skills required to produce a good feature interview. You can use it in one of two ways:

1 You can select a person to interview, set up the interview, carry it out, and then write it up. This is the better approach, but it takes a lot of organising. If you do this, you start work on page 174 with 'Finding your victim'.
2 You can use the interview transcripts in 'A spell in Africa'. If you do this, you start work on page 176 with 'Before you start'.

Standard Grade English – Credit

Finding your victim

Local heroes

Richard and Angela were lucky; they had the opportunity of interviewing a world champion boxer. But even if you don't happen to know someone famous to interview, it is surprising what fascinating stories can arise from interviewing apparently 'ordinary' people. Here are some suggestions:

School
- a retiring teacher looking back
- a new teacher looking forward
- or both as a contrast
- a parent with an unusual job
- a parent who helps to run a community scheme
- an ex-pupil remembering what the school was like in the past
- a visitor to the school.

Friends and family
- someone with an unusual job
- someone who has just come back from a foreign holiday
- an older person who can remember what life was like fifty years ago
- someone who has moved to the area in the recent past and who can tell you about the place where they used to live and how different it was.

The local community
You may know someone with a specific job that gives them a particular view of your local community:

- librarian
- traffic warden
- supermarket manager
- council worker
- market stallholder.

Making the approach

People react in different ways to being asked for an interview. Most people are quite flattered to be asked and, once they have got over any nervousness, enjoy the experience of talking about their lives and experiences. It is important, however, to approach them in the right way.

Face to face
If it is someone you know quite well, then the obvious thing to do is to call on them and just ask. But even with someone you know very well, don't forget to tell them what the interview is for and what your questions will be about. (See Bare bones below.)

By letter
If it is a person you do not know – or do not know very well – you may prefer to make the first approach by letter. In this case it is even more important to make sure you explain the Bare bones of the interview. Since this is a school project, you may want to tell the person that the interview is being set up as part of your work in English and give them the name of your teacher. (It is a good idea to ask your English teacher to check your letter before sending it.)

Bare bones

Whichever approach you use, it is important to make sure that the person understands:

- **what** you want to interview them about
- **why** you are doing it
- **when** (roughly) you need to do the interview
- **where** it will take place. (Some people are happy to be interviewed at home; in other cases you may have to arrange to interview them at school – this will need to be organised with your teacher.)
- **how long** you think it will take; an hour should be long enough for a short feature article.

Preparation

Good interviewing

Research

Before you start working out what questions to ask, you should do some preliminary research. Otherwise you may miss the opportunity of asking *just* the right question to open up a really interesting story. Collect as much background information as you can about the person you are going to interview and the experiences you are going to ask about. There are three possible sources for this:

- your own knowledge and experience; just sitting and thinking carefully about the topic will often suggest possible lines
- asking other people; if your subject is a local one, friends and family will often be able to supply information
- books and magazines; the school or local library will often be able to provide useful additional background information.

Technicalities

When you have prepared carefully for an interview, you want to be sure that you come away from it with a detailed record of what was said. By far the best way of doing this is to:

- use a tape recorder
- make written notes as well.

The tape recorder

Remember: if something *can* go wrong – *it will*!

- Practise using the tape recorder until you can almost use it blindfold.
- Make sure that if it works on batteries, it has new ones in it.
- If it is a mains-powered machine, make sure that you have the lead, and an extension cable.

Making written notes

Keep your notes as brief as possible, but:

- make sure you can read them
- write out in full any statements you want to quote and any names that may be difficult to spell.

Questions

You should aim to have a list of questions prepared and written down. A good interviewer does not keep referring to this list, but always has one. Making a list like this has three main values:

- it makes you sort out your ideas and plan the interview in advance
- it helps you out if – as can happen – your mind suddenly goes blank
- it is useful towards the end of the interview; you can check to make sure that you have not missed out anything important.

Prepare your list like this:

1 Write down the main topics you want to cover.
2 For each topic brainstorm all the possible questions to ask.
3 Sort your questions into a sensible sequence.
4 Make a neat and very clear copy of your questions; you need to be able to read it quickly.

Conducting the interview

- Do your best to make the person you are interviewing feel at ease – take some time to talk to them generally before beginning the interview.
- Don't feel you have to stick to your list of prepared questions. Be ready to add follow-up questions if you get an answer that is interesting or unexpected.
- When you have finished, remember to thank the person and don't just rush off. Take time, again, to talk to them politely, before leaving.

Before you start

It is always helpful to look at how other people set about writing an interview feature. On the next two pages are the interviews that Richard and Angela did, printed as they actually appeared. Read them and then follow the instructions on this page.

We can build a better world

What questions do you think Richard asked Steve Robinson? It is possible to work some of them out by reading his article carefully:

> Now living in Marshfield, Gwent, Steve was brought up in Bromley Drive, Ely, and first got involved in boxing at the age of nine.
>
> 'My older brother, Paul, was into boxing at the time and we used to have sparring sessions,' he said.
>
> 'At that time he always used to win.'

How old were you when you started boxing?

How did you start?

Who used to win?

Read the article again.

1 Make a list of other questions that you think Richard must have asked and, for each one, explain why.
2 Make a list of questions that you would have liked to ask Steve if you had been interviewing him.

Q and A

As you can see, the newspaper decided to present Angela's interview as a series of questions and answers.

1 Angela and Richard have approached their interviews in different ways. What would you say were the main differences between the kinds of questions they asked?
2 If you had been Angela, what other questions would you have wanted to ask Steve?

Now that you have looked at interviews by other people, look back at your own list of questions and see if it needs altering in any way.

Do your interview.

STICK AT IT: Champ's message

'We can build a better world'

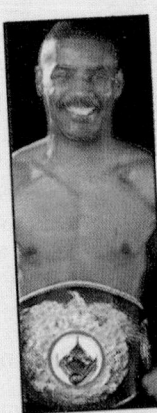

Steve Robinson

As Wales' world champion boxer Steve Robinson went back to his old, **Glyn Derw High School**, in Ely, Cardiff, to promote BT Environment Week '95, pupil **RICHARD COLLINS** seized the opportunity to interview him about his school days and career

ON a wet Monday morning, Glyn Derw High School, in Ely, Cardiff, welcomed a world champion and released 250 pink heart shaped balloons into the sky as BT announced its environment week.

Steve Robinson, 26, is the featherweight champion of the world, a media megastar and, more importantly, an ex-Glyn Derw pupil.

Now living in Marshfield, Gwent, Steve was brought up in Bromley Drive, Ely, and first got involved in boxing at the age of nine.

"My older brother, Paul, was into boxing at the time and we used to have sparring sessions" he said.

"At that time he always used to win."

Boxing has come in for a lot of criticism recently, but Steve defends it as a sport, claiming it keeps boys off the streets and gives them a sense of self-worth when they are perhaps failing in other areas.

He believes that everyone needs to get that kind of discipline and if, through training hard and showing dedication in the gym, you can gain this, then it is truly a worthy achievement.

At 24, Steve first made the headlines when, against expectations, he became Welsh Boxing champion. From then he has gone on to even greater things and is now World Champion, a title he intends to keep.

Yet such fame has not gone to his head. The first thing you notice about Steve Robinson is a shy, warm smile and a complete lack of arrogance.

He is a family man who cherishes the time spent with his two young sons and cares about people and the world around him. A regular visitor to Glyn Derw, he sets a great example to pupils and is well chosen to promote interest in the environment.

"The world around us is important and we can all do something to preserve and improve our environment," said Steve.

"Young children can help by picking up litter; teenagers can do gardening for elderly neighbours. Little things like that are important and if we all stick at it we can be successful."

Steve has shown how "sticking at it" leads to success. Glyn Derw pupils will respond to BT's call to do their best for the environment. We hope the message spreads.

● Steve Robinson Question and Answer: Page 3
● BT Environment Week competition: Page 3

Q and A

STEVE ROBINSON had for long been someone I respected and admired, not just as a boxer, but as a person fame and fortune could never change.

Interviewing a star was not easy and I don't suppose being interviewed was either. We were both very nervous but Steve's manager, Ronnie Rush, put us at our ease and everything went smoothly. Here are some of the questions I asked Steve about his school life:

Q How did you feel about school?

A I enjoyed school. I thought it was all right.

Q Were there any lessons you were particularly good at?

A Sport. I loved sport and I never forgot my PE kit. I thought I was a good sportsman, even as a kid.

Q Do you have any regrets?

A Yes. I regret taking a break from boxing. If I hadn't taken a break and kept on boxing then maybe I could have won the World Boxing Organisation Featherweight title at an earlier age.

Q Did you have any ambitions to become anything other than a boxer?

A No, I always wanted to be a boxer from the early age of nine. My brother, who is five years older than me, was already boxing, so I suppose I followed in his footsteps.

Q What advice would you give teenagers who, like you, want to leave school at an early age in search of a career in sport?

A Well, if they're really good at the sport and they think that they can do well, then they should go for it and don't let anyone stand in their way.

Q If your two boys wanted to leave school at an early age would you support their decision or encourage them to go back to school and further their education?

A I think I'd encourage them to go back to school, because I think an education is very important, especially these days.

Q While at school, what were your friends' reactions when you told them that you wanted to be a professional boxer?

A All my friends were boxing at the time so they didn't really say anything. I suppose they wanted to be boxers as well.

Q You have fulfilled one ambition in becoming a professional boxer. Do you have any other ambitions to follow?

A My only ambition is to settle down with my family and be happy. I think I'm a proper family man.

Apart from finding out about Steve's school life, I also found out he is 26, has a girlfriend and two sons. He used to live with his mother, Yvonne, until he moved out and went to live in Marshfield, Gwent.

As you can tell from reading this profile, he is an ordinary sort of man, who enjoys the simple things in life. He not only cares about himself and his family, but also other people and the environment.

Steve you are a great example for the younger generation to look up to in our modern day society. Well done.

Angela Coughlin,
Glyn Derw High School, Ely, Cardiff

Wales on Sunday

Practice

Coursework

Writing it up

This page contains advice on how to write up your interview. The examples are taken from Angela's interview on page 178.

Preparation

1 If you have a tape of the interview, listen to it once to get a general idea of what it contains. Listen to it again and make notes on the main topics covered. If the tape recorder has a counter, write down the counter numbers against these.

> 005 Feelings about school
>
> 032 Regrets
>
> 047 Ambitions

2 If you are working from written notes only, make a list of the main topics.

3 Decide which topics you want to include in your article. For each of these make more detailed notes on what was said in the interview.

> Feelings about school
> - enjoyed it: 'It was all right'
> - liked sport: 'I never forgot my PE kit'

4 Decide on the order in which you want to present the article.

> 1 School career
>
> 2 Getting into boxing
>
> 3 Ambitions then and now

Practice

Go through the stages above, using Angela's interview for practice.

Writing a first draft

When you have done this preparation, you are ready to write a first draft of your article.

Editing

In a newspaper or magazine, editing has two main purposes:

- to make an article clearer and easier to understand
- to shorten an article so that it will fit the space available.

There are four main ways in which an article can be edited.

1 By changing the order of sections, so that the whole article follows on in a way that is easier to understand, or more interesting.
2 By cutting out whole sections. This can only be done if the section you are cutting out stands on its own and does not have other parts of the article depending on it. In Richard's article, for example, this paragraph can be cut if necessary:

> *Yet such fame has not gone to his head. The first thing you notice about Steve Robinson is a shy, warm smile and a complete lack of arrogance.*

3 By cutting words or phrases. This is more likely to be possible than **2**, but it takes a lot of time and care. These examples are from Richard's article. The first shows light editing and the second heavier editing:

> *At 24, Steve first made the headlines when, ~~against expectations,~~ he became Welsh Boxing champion. From then he has gone on to even greater things and is now World Champion, ~~a title he intends to keep.~~*

> *At 24, Steve ~~first made the headlines when, against expectations,~~ he became Welsh Boxing champion. ~~From then he has gone on to even greater things~~ and is now World Champion, ~~a title he intends to keep.~~*

4 By rewriting. Sometimes this is the only way to shorten, or to make something clearer.

Practice

Imagine that you are the sub-editor. You have been told that there is only space to run Richard's article at about half the planned length. Edit it to about 150 words, trying to keep as much of the interest and flavour of the original as you can.

Your article

Now look again at your own first draft. The aim here is not to edit it for length, but to cut and change it so that it is as 'tight' and interesting as possible. When you are satisfied with it, make a fair copy.

B16 IN THE HEAT OF THE SUN

Voluntary Service Overseas is a development agency sending men and women to share their skills with people in over 55 developing countries. Since 1958, more than 20,000 volunteers have worked overseas with VSO.

See: ● **A2** Finding things (p8)
● **A3** Presentation of information (p10)
● **A16** Argument and persuasion (p49)
● **A19** Writing an article (p59)

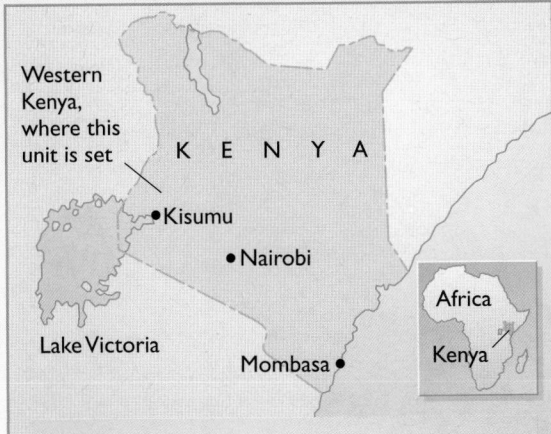

Western Kenya, where this unit is set

K E N Y A

● Kisumu
● Nairobi

Lake Victoria

Mombasa ●

Africa

Kenya

We visited three volunteers in Western Kenya to talk to them and the people they were working with and to take photographs of them at work. This unit is the result of that visit.

Born in Jamaica – came to Britain (aged 7) with parents – lived in Manchester until she was 17

'We carried out a health needs survey and found that there is a major problem of malnutrition here – particularly in the under-5s.'

The text
The unit contains three types of text:

■ explanatory text by us
■ datafiles in note form
■ direct quotations of what the three volunteers said.

The activities
There are short activities at intervals through the unit. These are designed to help you make sure you have understood fully. At the end of the unit, on page 192, there is a variety of longer writing activities suitable for coursework or examination practice.

The volunteers

Patsy Sterling

Born in Jamaica – came to Britain (aged 7) with parents – lived in Manchester until she was 17, then family moved to English Midlands – went to Aston University and took degree in Environmental Biology – went to London and did 3-year sandwich course in Environmental Health – worked as Environmental Health Officer in Lambeth for 3 years – moved to Wandsworth as Environmental Health Officer – after four years became dissatisfied with the 'stifling' nature of her work and so decided to apply to VSO.

Gavin Anderson

Comes from north-east Scotland – studied industrial design at Edinburgh – wanted to find out how his training could be used in developing countries – got university to sponsor him to go to Zimbabwe – was offered 2-year job with organisation which helped workers in manufacturing, metalworking and other crafts – advised craft workers on designing new products that would sell – returned to Britain and went to technical college and studied metal engineering – learned to weld – also joined blacksmithing workshop part time – after 16 months in Britain applied to VSO.

Rachel Yeats

Comes from north-east Scotland – studied textile design at Manchester – decided she did not want to follow normal career paths, but wanted to work with people – joined Gavin in Zimbabwe – helped train and advise local craftspeople making tapestries and wall-hangings, dolls, knitwear, and painting – returned to Britain and did a variety of things – worked in centre for adults with special needs – worked in weaving workshop – worked for a fair trade organisation, ordering crafts from developing countries for sale in Britain – after 16 months in Britain applied to VSO.

Preparation

A closer look

1 These datafiles were written up from information given at the beginning of the interviews with the volunteers. If you had been the interviewer, what questions would you have wanted to ask each of them?

2 Choose one of the three datafiles. Imagine that you are a journalist working for the local newspaper in the area where that volunteer lives. Write a short 'personal profile' to be published at the time they leave Britain.

Patsy Sterling: problems ...

Patsy Sterling was asked by the Kenyan YMCA in Indangalasia, Mumias District, Western Kenya, to help initiate a Primary Healthcare Programme. She began by conducting a survey of family health and found that economic developments in the area had led to unexpected difficulties, particularly in the area of nutrition.

In the past families had enough land to produce all the food they needed (subsistence farming) on the family smallholding ('shamba').

The staple food was maize which was taken off the cob and winnowed by hand. Most of the protein came from vegetables.

Money did not play an important part in people's lives. At the local market spare produce was sold and additional protein, such as dried fish, could be bought.

When sugar cane was introduced as a cash crop, families were encouraged to use their land to grow the cane and sell it to the factory at Mumias. In theory they could then use the money to buy food. But this caused problems.

Sugar cane takes two years from planting to harvest. At harvest time the growers are well paid, but the money they receive has to last two years. It is like having a good job for which your wages are only paid once every two years.

As a result many families gave over most of their land to sugar cane, but then found that they had problems in getting enough food for a healthy diet.

... and solutions

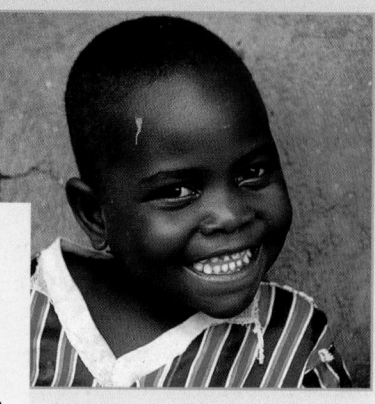

We carried out a health needs survey and found that there is a major problem of malnutrition here – particularly in the under-5s. There's a lot of hidden malnutrition, because all the children look healthy. It's only when you stand a malnourished child up against a child that is well-fed, that the differences
5 become apparent.

The land is very fertile. There's plenty of rainfall and the climate here is ideal for growing things all the year round. One of the things that we've had to do at the YMCA is not to say to people, 'Look: you've got to stop growing sugar cane.' We've had to look at other ways of encouraging them to grow the
10 things that they need to stay healthy. That's where organic farming came in.

The advantage of this form of farming is that it does not require expensive fertilisers but, properly done, makes it possible to get far more – and better – crops from the same amount of land.

The idea was that various types of organic vegetable beds would be set up so that the members of the community can actually come onto the site, see these beds, and learn how to make these beds for themselves. We grew common vegetables on a double-dug organic
5 bed next to a bit of land that was ploughed the traditional way. We planted vegetables like *sukuma wiki* (a kind of spinach) so they can see for themselves, and compare the growth on the two plots.

Patsy also encouraged the setting up of tree nurseries, so that farmers could grow their own replacement trees.

There are various species of trees that the farmer can use on his homestead not only to help to improve his soil, by acting as a windbreak, but also for fodder for the animals in the dry season. The idea is to encourage farmers to use
5 trees a lot more on their land. The main source of fuel in this rural area is trees: they're being used up at a very fast rate and they're not being replaced.

Preparation

Pages 183–184

There are four photographs on these two pages. For each one:

- Find a short quotation from the text to act as a caption.
- Write a caption or title in your own words.

Local people had been growing vegetables in the same way for generations. Why should they change? Imagine you are Patsy. How would you persuade them to change to this new method?

Fresh, clean water

Another health problem Patsy became aware of was that although there are plenty of natural springs in the area, most of them do not provide healthy drinking water.

The YMCA asked her to start a spring protection scheme. She decided to start with a pilot scheme to protect three of the 48 springs in the district. She was determined, however, that this project should involve the local communities at every stage. If they wanted springs protected, they must:

- form a committee to be responsible for the work
- provide all the necessary materials that were locally available (rocks, sand, timber)
- pay for the wages of the labourers who would do a lot of the work
- learn how to protect other springs, by working on the pilot project themselves.

For its part, the YMCA would:

- provide specialist materials like waterproof cement and iron piping
- get the necessary permissions from the local authority
- organise the craftsman who would teach the villagers what was involved.

Questions

1 Look at the photograph of an unprotected spring and see if you can work out what the health problems are. (Remember that most families in the area have cattle and goats.)
2 What are the main differences you can see in the picture of a protected spring? Why would it be healthier?
3 What would be the advantages of insisting that the local community did the things that Patsy asked?

An unprotected spring

A protected spring

Black mzungu

> There are positives and negatives to being a black person here. For example, the Kenyans all think that I'm a Kenyan, which is nice, but the downside is that they expect me to speak the
> 5 various Kenyan languages.
>
> Locally, people know I'm a stranger. The fact that I ride around on a motorcycle and am a woman is blowing quite a few people's minds. I don't act or behave the same way as the other
> 10 women do here. I live on my own in a house. I don't have any children, I don't have a husband: therefore I'm a 'Miss' and I'm 'missing' – that's the local term. Even if I didn't open my mouth they'll know I'm a stranger, but they'll still react
> 15 to me differently than they do to the whites who they call mzungus here.
>
> They seem to expect more from me as a fellow black person. When they see me, they see an African and their expectations are completely
> 20 different. If I'm in the market and they've told me it's ten shillings for a cabbage and I know it's only five shillings, I want to give them five shillings. They get very upset because they feel somehow that I'm doing them out of this five
> 25 shillings. But if I'd been a mzungu and I'd bartered them down to five shillings they would have great respect for me. They see me as a black mzungu.
>
> They've accepted me, but in differing ways.
> 30 The older men accept me as an honorary male because I do not act the same way as the women. The things that I do – riding a motorcycle, managing a project, going out and being outspoken with the chief or other people in
> 35 power – are male things. So their way of accepting me is to treat me as an honorary male.
>
> It was very interesting when my parents came here last November, to see the villagers' reaction – particularly to the relationship between my mother and my father. My mother will tell my father off for something – which is
> 40 unheard of here – and she'll tell him to go and do something. The women don't boss the men around here; it's the other way round. They somehow expected my parents to be mzungus, to be white. Even though I'd shown them photographs etc. they still couldn't comprehend.

Question

You're living on your own in this tiny little house. You haven't got any electricity. You haven't got any hot water. You're all on your own in the middle of nowhere, and you get hardly any money. So … why are you doing it?

Answer

I'm doing it because I believe in what VSO is doing. Their idea is to facilitate people
5 sharing skills, ideas, knowledge with people from a developing country. Volunteers learn new ideas and skills that we can also use when we get back home. I felt that although I have a lot to give, there was also a lot that I wanted to learn, and I wanted to find out what it's like being in a situation where I'm totally on my own. I have to rely on myself for company, entertainment. This particular job is unstructured so I've got to put some
10 kind of structure to whatever I'm doing. It was a challenge and I think I've risen to the challenge quite well. I've learned a lot about myself.

Preparation

Questions

1 What are the disadvantages Patsy finds in being a black volunteer in Kenya?
2 What does she mean by calling herself a 'black mzungu'?
3 In what ways do local people find it challenging that she is a woman?
4 Which aspects of Patsy's life and work would you find most challenging and most rewarding?

Research

Patsy says that volunteers learn new ideas and skills that they can use when they get back home. Bearing in mind her training and experience in Britain, what new ideas and skills will she take back with her?

Rachel and Gavin: with the Jua Kali

Gavin and Rachel were given a placement in Kisumu, a large town on the shores of Lake Victoria. They were to work with a group of people known as the *Jua Kali*. Gavin explains what this means:

Kenya is a country that's going through a lot of changes. In the past it was a very agriculturally-based country with a fast-growing population. A lot of people have moved into urban areas but the amount of industry hasn't grown with the urban population. So a lot of people drift into what is known as the Jua Kali sector to find jobs.

5   Jua Kali is Kiswahili: *Jua* is the word for 'sun' amd *kali* is the word for 'hot' or 'fierce'. When they say the 'Jua Kali sector' they mean the people who work in the hot fierce sun, people who are – say – metalworkers, tinsmiths, carpenters, textile workers – a real variety of people.

   They have no proper accommodation; they work in small shacks in the sun, doing manufacturing activities. It's a very large sector in Kenya, which provides a lot of employment to Kenyans.

10   Many of the people in the Jua Kali don't have the finance or enough money to actually invest in new materials. So metalworkers, for example, will try and find scrap metal to work with – metal that's come from industry that's just waste … tinsmiths will find things like tin cans which they will flatten out and re-use. Even tools that the Jua Kali people use tend to be made from scrap metal. For example they use hammers that are made from springs from vehicles.

15   One of the big problems with the Jua Kali is that they produce – a lot of people produce – the same product so they're really competing with each other. For example there's the jiko, which is a stove which people cook on. In Jua Kali there may be sixty workshops producing the same jiko. The only thing they have to compete on is price. So they beat each other's price lower and lower.

K.I.C.K.

Rachel is the Crafts Adviser and Gavin is the Technical Adviser at the Kisumu Innovation Centre, Kenya. K.I.C.K aims to help people in the Jua Kali to use their skills in order to earn a better living.

They do this by:

- suggesting different products to open up new markets
- providing technical advice
- helping with quality control
- giving business advice
- providing affordable office facilities.

Case study

1 Too many tinsmiths making jikos: too much competition driving prices down.

2 K.I.C.K advising them on using skills to make different products.

3 Materials available: sheet metal rejected by companies making cocoa tins, shoe polish tins, and similar items.

4 One group making office equipment: desk tidies, filing card boxes, document cases from this waste metal.

5 Started by painting the metal to cover up company logos printed on it.

6 K.I.C.K advised them that products with famous logos are now very fashionable.

7 Group now very successful marketing desk equipment and document cases with famous logos: Cadbury, Coca Cola, Kiwi.

8 K.I.C.K succeeded in selling these products into new markets, including back to Coca Cola etc as company gifts!

Gavin

'People are so enthusiastic – they get quite excited about developing new things. They are very sociable: people will come into the office just for a social visit. I feel I've been accepted into Jua Kali and I think that's very positive.

Working on the design of a new water carrier with David Osura

Advising Peter Onjiko of Inland Rural Technology on welding equipment

Rachel

> I think it's surprising that somebody can come from such a different culture and be accepted so easily. It's quite amazing the way that the Jua Kali have accepted us. I'll go back with enduring feelings of that.

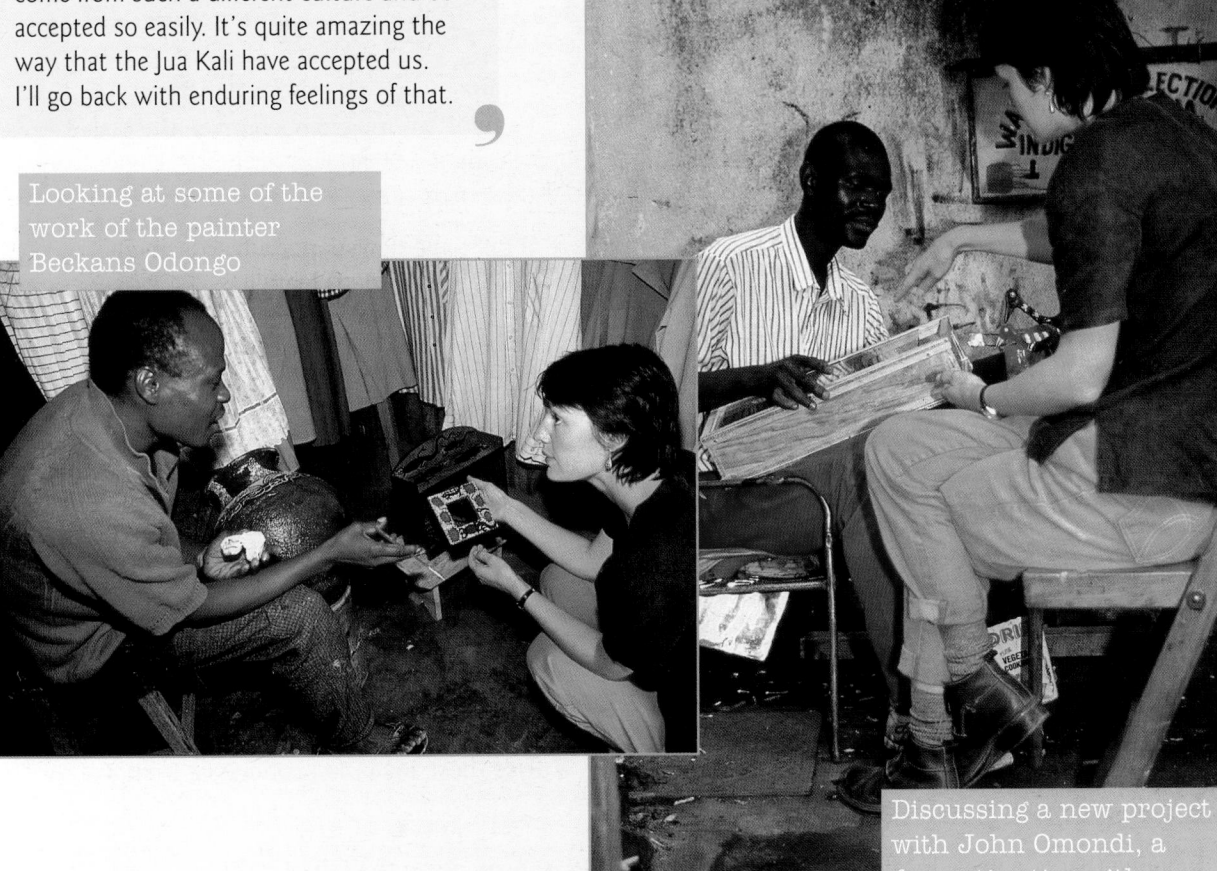

Looking at some of the work of the painter Beckans Odongo

Discussing a new project with John Omondi, a decorative tinsmith

Preparation

Pages 188–189

1 Read the text on page 188 carefully.
2 Write one or two sentences in answer to each of these questions:

   - What is the Jua Kali?
   - Why has it developed?

3 Write a short explanation of why people in the Jua Kali face difficulties selling their products.
4 Read the text on page 189.
5 Write a short paragraph explaining how and why K.I.C.K. helped the tinsmiths.

Pages 190–191

What new information do you find in these two pages about:

- Jua Kali?
- the different kinds of work done by Rachel and Gavin?
- their personalities and their response to the work they are doing in Kenya?

Activities

Talking points

1 In its statement of aims, VSO emphasises 'sharing skills'. What skills does each of the three volunteers described in this unit bring to Kenya?

2 What other personal qualities do you think the three of them show? (You can work out an answer to this question in three ways:

- from what they say
- from what they have done
- from the qualities they *must* have had in order to work in the situation that is described.)

3 What do you think would be the best things about doing this kind of work?

4 What would the worst things be?

5 On balance, would you find doing VSO attractive or unattractive, and why?

Practice

Coursework

Newspaper profile

Imagine that you are a local newspaper reporter and have been given the job of writing a full profile on one of these three volunteers on their return home from Kenya. You have all the information in this unit to draw on, including the photographs. Write an article of about 150–200 words and select two or three photographs to illustrate it. Give your article a suitable title.

Feature article

VSO has been the subject of many magazine and newspaper articles. This unit has given you the material for a similar article. It is possible to present the work and lives of volunteers in many different ways, according to the type of publication for which you are writing.

1 Choose a magazine for which you are going to write an article; take one from the list or think of a magazine that you know.

2 Decide whether you are going to write about all three volunteers or are going to be more selective.

3 Select the material you want to use. Make notes.

4 Choose the illustrations you will use. You can have between two and five. Give each one a caption.

5 Write your article.

Practice

Coursework

Advertising VSO

VSO depends on charitable donations for part of its funds. You have been given the task of preparing a new appeal for funds. Choose one of these formats:

- a full page newspaper advertisement
- an A5 (A4 folded) leaflet
- a 60-second radio advertisement.

You have been given the material about Rachel, Gavin and Patsy to form the basis of your appeal.

1 Think about the main aims of VSO and about *why* they need the money and *how* they will spend it.

2 Think about the work done by Patsy, Rachel and Gavin. How do you think the Kenyans at K.I.C.K. and the YMCA feel about the contribution that these three volunteers are making?

3 Use these ideas to produce your appeal.

Magazines
- a popular magazine
- a serious environmental or geographical magazine
- a magazine for teenagers
- a magazine for retired people